practical typography from a to Z

Poynter Institute for Media Studies
Library

SEP 1 6 '86

By Frank Romano

Published by the National Composition Association
a special industry group of Printing Industries of America, Inc.

Produced in conjunction with

Typographers Association of New York

Published by
The National Composition Association
1730 North Lynn Street
Arlington, Virginia 22209

© 1983 Frank J. Romano
All rights reserved.
Reproduction in whole or part
by any means without specific written
permission is prohibited.

Table of Contents

Accents	2	Hairline	66
Agate	5	Hyphenation	67
Alignment	6	Homographs	69
Alphabet Length	8	Ideograph	72
Alternate Characters	12	Indention	73
Ampersand	14	Inline	74
Apex	15	Initial	78
Arrows	16	Italic	79
Ascender	17	Justification	82
Biform	20	Kerning	84
Blackletter	21	Leaders	88
Book Typography	22	Legibility	90
Borders	24	Letterspacing	91
Boxes and Bullets	25	Ligature	93
Bracketed	26	Line Length	94
Brush	27	Line Spacing	95
Calligraphy	30	Logo	97
Capitals	31	Lowercase	98
Cap Line	32	Magnetic Ink Characters	102
Closed	33	Math	103
Color, Typographic	34	Newspaper Typography	108
Condensed	35	Optical Spacing	110
Contour	36	Ornaments	112
Contrast	38	Outline	113
Copperplate	39	Paragraphs	116
Counter	40	Percent	117
Cyrillic	41	Phonetics	118
Dashes	44	Pi	119
Digitized Typography	46	Pictograph	121
Ellipses	50	Point System	122
Emphasis	51	Proof Marks	123
Expanded	52	Proportional	125
Figures	54	Punctuation	126
Fixed Space	54	Quadding	130
Font	57	Quotes	131
Footnotes and References	58	Ragged	134
Format	59	Reference Marks	136
Fractions	60	Roman	137
Galley	62	Sans Serif	140
Greek	63	Script	142
Gutter	64		

Serif	143
Set Width	144
Shaded	145
Small Cap	146
Stem	147
Stress	148
Superior/Inferior	149
Symmetry	150
Tabular	152
Terminal	153
Trap	154
Type Series	155
Type Size	156
Uncial	162
Unit System	163
Vertical Setting	168
Weight	170
Word Space	171
x-height	174
Index	175

a

Accents

Agate

Alignment

Alphabet Length

Alternate Characters

Ampersand

Apex

Arrows

Ascender

Accents

Originally, this term meant "accented characters"—that is, the combination of a character *and* its appropriate accent—such as the ñ, pronounced as *'ny'* in Spanish or the ç, pronounced as an *'s'* in French. The accents in these examples, the tilde and the cedila, combine with the character to form a specialized character, primarily for pronunciation and foreign language use.

Today, most accented characters do not exist as a single unit, but are formed by combining characters and accents. The accents most often used are:

Acute	é
Angstrom	å
Breve (or Macron)	ā
Cedila	ç
Circumflex	ô
Dieresis (also called an Umlaut)	ö
Grave	è
Short	ā
Tilde	ñ
Umlaut (also called a Dieresis)	ö

The accent is stored as a separate character in most cases, with zero width (no escapement value). Thus, it "floats" above or below a character position. Accents used in this manner are designed for the weight, style and height (cap and lowercase) of a typeface.

$$' + e = é$$

There are two methods for keying accented characters: either an individual key indicating the complete character, or two separate keys, one for the accent and one for the character. In this latter case, the output device selects the accent, positions it with no escapement, then positions the character, which escapes normally.

Because of the height limitation of some output devices, the caps may be shortened to allow for accent space.

In hot metal there was a special problem that is reflected in the examples below. The first is a standard character plus accent—but a high-cap mold was needed. Normally to avoid cost and time, a slightly reduced character was used so that the additional height of the accent equalled the cap height. We do not have this problem today, but you may encounter settings like this and someone may ask you to "match" it. Tell them that it was a limitation of hot metal.

The accented caps are smaller than unaccented caps— a hot metal limitation.

DU METAL DES CARACTÈRES

DU MÉTAL DES CARACTÈRES

Here are the accents used in those languages that use English alphabetic characters:

Albanian
Á Ç É Ë Ê Í Ó Ú Ý
á ç é ë ê í ó ú ý

Anglo-Saxon
Ā Æ Ð Ē Ę Ʒ Ī Ō Þ Ǫ Ū Ȳ
ā æ ð ē ę ʒ ī ō þ ǫ ū ȳ

Basque
Ç D̄ L̄ Ñ Ŕ Š T̄ Ü
ç d̄ ī ñ ŕ š t̄ ü

Basque-Spanish
D̄ L̄ Ñ Ŕ Š T̄ Ü
d̄ ī ñ ŕ š t̄ ü

Basque-French
Ç D̄ L̄ Ñ Ŕ Š T̄ Ü
ç d̄ ī ñ ŕ š t̄ ü

Boheminan (Czech.)
Á Č Ď É Ě Í Ň Ó Ř Š T̆
Ú Ů Ý Ž á č d' é ě í ň ó ř
š t' ú ů ý ž

Catalan
À Ç É È Í Ï Ó Ú Ü L·L
à ç é è í ï ó ò ú ü l·l

Danish
Å Ø å é ø

Dutch
â ä à ë é è ê ì ï ó ò ô ö
ù û ü ij

Esperanto
Ĉ Ĝ Ĥ Ĵ Ŝ Ŭ ĉ ĝ ĥ ĵ ŝ ŭ

Estonian
Ä Ö Õ Ü ä ö õ ü

Finnish
Ä Å Ö ä å ö

Flemish
â ä à ë é è ê ì ï ó ò ô ö
ù û ü ij

French
À Â Ç É È Ê Ë Î Ï Ô
Ù Û Ü
à â ç é è ê ë î ï ô ù û ü

Frisian
Â Ê Ô Ú Û â ê ô ú û

German
Ä Ö Ü ä ö ü

Hungarian
Á É Í Ó Ö Ő Ú Ü Ű
á é í ó ö ő ú ü ű

3̄

Icelandic (Modern)
Á Ð É Í Ó Ö Þ Ú Ý
á ð é í ó ö þ ú ý

Islandic (Old)
Á E Ð É Í Ó Ǫ Ǫ́ Ø Ǿ Þ
Ú Ý á æ ð é í ó ǫ ǫ́ ø ǿ þ ú ý

Italian
À È Ì Î Ò Ù à è ì î ò ù

Latin   Turkish
Ğ İ Ş Ö ğ ı ş ö

Lettish
Ā Č Ē Ģ Ī Ķ Ļ Ņ Ŗ Š Ū Ž
ā č ē ģ ī ķ ļ ņ ŗ š ū ž

Lithuanian
Ą Č Ė Ę Į Š Ū Ų Ž
ą č ė ę į š ū ų ž

Norweigian
Å Ø å á é ǫ́ ø

Polish
Ą Ć Ę Ł Ń Ó Ś Ź Ż
ą ć ę ł ń ó ś ź ż

Portuguese
Á Ã Ç É Ê Í Ó Ô Õ Ú
á ã ç é ê í ó ô õ ú

Romansh
Â Ā Ê Ē É Î Ô Ö Ü
â ā ê ē é î ô ö ü

Roumanian
Â Ă À È Î Ì Ò Ş Ţ Ù
â ă à è î ì ò ş ţ ù

Russian
İ Ë Ў ё ў

Serbo-Croatian
(Yugo-Slav)
Ć Č Đ Š Ž ć č đ š ž

Slovakian
Á Á Č Ď É Í Ľ Ĺ Ň Ô Ŕ
Š Ť Ú Ý Ž á ä č ď é í ľ ĺ
ň ô ŕ š ť ú ý ž

Slovenian
Č S Ž č š ž

Spanish
Á É Í Ñ Ó Ú Ü
á é í ñ ó ú ü

Swedish
Å Ä Ö å ä ö

Tagalog
Á É Ġ Í Ń Ó Ú á à â é è ê
ġ í ì î ñ ó ò ô ú ù û

Tamil (Roman)
Ḥ Ḳ Ḷ Ḹ Ṃ Ṁ Ṇ Ṅ Ṉ
Ṛ Ṣ ḥ ḳ ḷ ḹ ṃ ṁ ṇ ṅ ṉ ṛ ṣ

Urdu (Roman)
Ā Ą CH Ḍ DH Ē GN Ḥ Ḥ
Ī Ḳ KH Ṅ Ñ Ō Ṛ Ṣ Ṣ SH
Ṭ Ṭ TH Ū Z Ẓ ZH ā ą
ch ḍ dh ē gn ḥ ḥ ī ḳ kh ṅ
n̄ ō ṛ ṣ ṣ sh t̤ ṭ th ū z ẓ zh

Welsh
Â Ê Î Ô Ŵ Ŷ â à è ê ë
î ï ì ô ò ö û ŵ ŷ ỳ

Weltervreden, Java
(Dutch East Indies)
á à â ä ç é è ê ë í ì î ñ
ó ò ô ö ú ù û ü ij

Yugo-Slav
(See Serbo-Croatian)

Agate

Originally, the sizes of type were expressed in names, not numbers. The name for 5½-point was Agate and it is still used today to describe the point size often used in newspaper classified advertising.

Newspapers also use "agate" as a unit of measurement for display advertising. There are 14 "agate" lines in 1 inch. Ad rates are usually "per line, per column." Thus a 2-column, 2-inch ad would be 56 "lines" (2 × 14 × 2 = 56).

Classified ads, or "liners," are separated by rule lines.

The column width depends upon the newspaper or publication. To save money, many newspapers keep narrowing the width of their sheets, thus modifying column measures. Never assume a column width; always confirm its value.

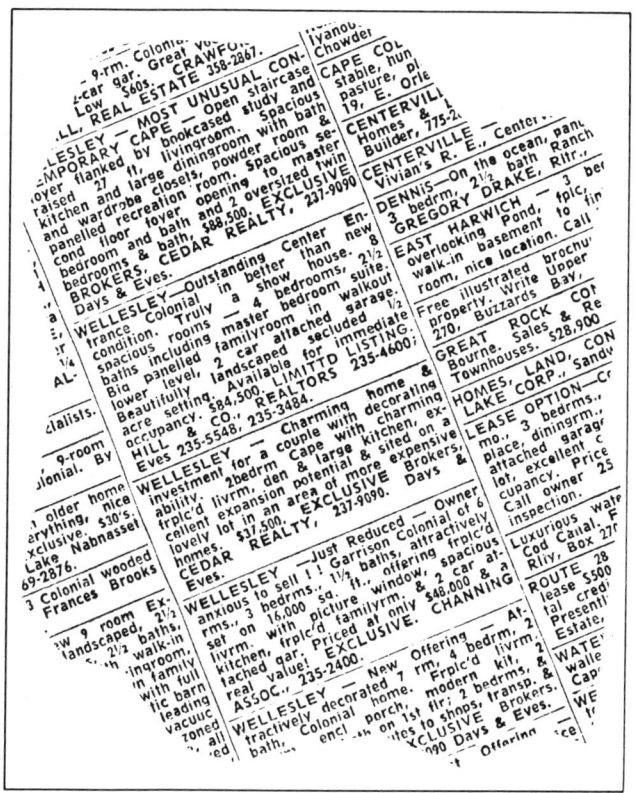

Alignment

All typefaces and size variations align on an imaginary horizontal reference line, called a baseline.

Baseline **M** M M M M

This alignment is necessary so that all styles and sizes can be mixed in the same line.

Horizontal alignment is based on the baseline.

Vertical alignment is based on the margins.

Machines can only align items according to pre-set reference points; thus, the need for human review for optical alignment.

For character alignment, the following groupings apply:

Baseline: f h i k l m n r x z fi fl ff ffi ffl
Top of m: m g o p q
Top of o: a b c d e s t u
Top of x: v w y
Top of i: j
Baseline: A B D E F H I K L M N P R T X Y Z
Top of H: J U V W
Bottom of U: C G O S
Top of O: Q

Optical alignment involves the use of some visual "reference" point. For instance, in the setting of vertical lines, characters would not be flushed left but rather centered:

Even if you do it correctly, avoid vertical setting.

Flush Left	**Centered**
V	V
E	E
R	R
T	T
I	I
C	C
A	A
L	L

Optical alignment may also require that curved or angular characters be slightly off center to achieve "visual" alignment.

These letters don't look right but they are geometrically correct . . .

These letters do look right, but the alignment is changed slightly . . .

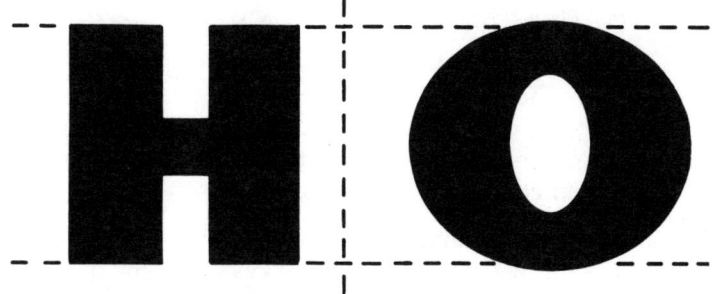

Alphabet Length

The alphabet used here is the lowercase *a through z* for any typeface. By comparing the length of these letters (when set normally in the same size) for different typefaces, one can evaluate comparative "mass." A typeface with a low alphabet length would set more characters in the same space than a typeface with a high alphabet length. This same relationship is also expressed as "characters per pica" (CPP)—the number of characters that fit in one pica.

Sometimes alphabet length is expressed in the relative units of the typesetting machine. The comparative capability still exists.

Character count is the average number of characters per line multiplied by the total lines.

Characters Per Line = CCP × Line Length

To arrive at a character count, count characters individually or measure your lines to the nearest inch and multiply this figure by the number of characters per inch (assuming you are counting typewritten copy). The *pica* typewriter has large characters (10 per inch); the *elite* typewriter has smaller characters (12 per inch).

Establish an average line length and draw a vertical line through your copy at that point. Establish the number of characters up to the line. Count the number of lines on your page and multiply this figure by the number of characters per line. This will give you an approximate count only. When extreme accuracy is necessary, count the number of characters extending beyond your vertical line and add this number. *You have now established your character count.*

Next: determine the style and size of the type that you are going to use and the line length in picas.

Find the typeface and the size that you are going to use in a copyfitting chart. Multiply the line length you are using *times* the characters per pica figure for the typeface you have selected. This will give you the amount of characters per line. Now divide the total character count by the characters per line figure. This tells you how many lines of copy you have. Then: multiply the number of typeset lines times the leading you have selected, which will result in your copy depth in points. (There are 12 points to a pica, 6 picas to an inch.)

TYPEFACE NAME	CHARACTERS PER PICA												
	6	7	8	9	10	11	12	14	18	24	30	36	48	60	72
American Classic Medium	3.64	3.12	2.73	2.42	2.19	1.98	1.82	1.56	1.21	.91	.73	.61	.45	.36	.30
American Classic Italic	3.64	3.12	2.73	2.42	2.19	1.98	1.82	1.56	1.21	.91	.73	.61	.45	.36	.30
American Classic Bold	3.42	2.96	2.58	2.30	2.07	1.87	1.71	1.48	1.15	.86	.69	.57	.43	.34	.29
American Classic Extrabold	3.40	2.92	2.55	2.28	2.04	1.86	1.70	1.46	1.14	.85	.68	.57	.43	.34	.28
American Typewriter Light	3.88	3.32	2.92	2.59	2.33	2.12	1.94	1.66	1.29	.97	.77	.64	.48	.38	.32
American Typewriter Medium	3.88	3.32	2.92	2.59	2.33	2.12	1.94	1.66	1.29	.97	.77	.64	.48	.38	.32
American Typewriter Bold	3.88	3.32	2.92	2.59	2.33	2.12	1.94	1.66	1.29	.97	.77	.64	.48	.38	.32
Antique Olive Light	4.12	3.53	3.09	2.74	2.47	2.24	2.06	1.76	1.37	1.03	.82	.69	.51	.41	.34
Antique Olive Medium	3.65	3.13	2.74	2.44	2.19	1.99	1.83	1.57	1.22	.91	.73	.61	.46	.37	.30
Antique Olive Bold	3.41	2.92	2.55	2.27	2.04	1.86	1.70	1.46	1.14	.85	.68	.57	.43	.34	.28
Antique Olive Compact	3.01	2.57	2.25	2.00	1.80	1.64	1.49	1.28	1.01	.75	.60	.50	.37	.30	.25
Avant Garde Light	4.11	3.53	3.08	2.74	2.47	2.24	2.06	1.76	1.37	1.03	.82	.68	.51	.41	.34
Avant Garde Book	4.00	3.42	2.99	2.66	2.40	2.18	2.00	1.71	1.33	1.00	.80	.66	.50	.40	.33
Avant Garde Medium	3.92	3.36	2.94	2.61	2.35	2.14	1.96	1.67	1.30	.97	.78	.65	.48	.39	.32
Avant Garde Bold	3.71	3.18	2.78	2.47	2.23	2.02	1.85	1.59	1.23	.92	.74	.61	.46	.37	.30
Aura	4.92	4.20	3.69	3.26	2.94	2.68	2.46	2.10	1.63	1.23	.98	.82	.61	.49	.41
Baskerville Medium	4.62	3.97	3.47	3.09	2.78	2.52	2.31	1.98	1.54	1.16	.92	.77	.58	.46	.38
Baskerville Italic	5.49	4.70	4.12	3.66	3.29	2.99	2.74	2.35	1.83	1.37	1.09	.91	.68	.54	.45
Baskerville Bold	4.31	3.69	3.23	2.87	2.59	2.35	2.16	1.85	1.44	1.08	.86	.77	.54	.43	.38
Benguiat Book	3.90	3.34	2.93	2.60	2.34	2.13	1.95	1.67	1.30	.98	.78	.65	.49	.39	.33
Benguiat Medium	3.83	3.28	2.87	2.55	2.29	2.09	1.91	1.64	1.27	.96	.76	.64	.48	.38	.32
Benguiat Bold	3.48	2.98	2.61	2.32	2.09	1.90	1.74	1.49	1.16	.87	.70	.58	.43	.35	.29
Bodoni Book	4.84	4.16	3.63	3.23	2.91	2.64	2.42	2.07	1.61	1.21	.97	.80	.60	.48	.40
Bodoni Book Italic	4.84	4.16	3.63	3.23	2.91	2.64	2.42	2.07	1.61	1.21	.97	.80	.60	.48	.40
Bodoni Bold	4.13	3.54	3.10	2.75	2.48	2.25	2.06	1.77	1.37	1.03	.82	.68	.51	.41	.34
Bodoni Extrabold	3.32	2.84	2.50	2.22	2.00	1.82	1.66	1.42	1.11	.83	.66	.55	.41	.33	.27
Bodoni Extrabold Italic	3.32	2.84	2.50	2.22	2.00	1.82	1.66	1.42	1.11	.83	.66	.55	.41	.33	.27
Bodoni Extrabold Condensed	7.12	6.10	5.34	4.74	4.29	3.88	3.56	3.05	2.37	1.78	1.43	1.19	.89	.71	.59
Bookman Light	3.85	3.30	2.89	2.57	2.31	2.10	1.93	1.65	1.28	.96	.77	.64	.48	.39	.32
Bookman Light Italic	3.78	3.24	2.84	2.52	2.27	2.06	1.90	1.62	1.26	.95	.76	.63	.47	.38	.32
Bookman Medium	3.65	3.13	2.74	2.43	2.19	1.99	1.82	1.56	1.22	.91	.73	.61	.46	.37	.30
Bookman Italic	3.55	3.04	2.66	2.37	2.13	1.94	1.78	1.52	1.18	.89	.71	.59	.44	.35	.30
Bookman Bold	3.39	2.91	2.54	2.26	2.04	1.85	1.70	1.45	1.13	.85	.68	.57	.42	.34	.28
Century Textbook	4.08	3.48	3.05	2.70	2.44	2.23	2.04	1.74	1.35	1.02	.81	.67	.51	.40	.33
Century Italic	4.08	3.48	3.05	2.70	2.44	2.23	2.04	1.74	1.35	1.02	.81	.67	.51	.40	.33
Century Bold	3.96	3.40	2.97	2.64	2.37	2.16	1.98	1.70	1.32	.99	.79	.66	.50	.40	.33
Cheltenham Light	4.75	4.07	3.56	3.17	2.85	2.59	2.38	2.04	1.58	1.19	.95	.79	.59	.48	.40
Cheltenham Light Italic	4.76	4.09	3.57	3.18	2.86	2.60	2.38	2.04	1.59	1.19	.95	.79	.60	.48	.40
Cheltenham Book	4.50	3.85	3.37	2.99	2.70	2.45	2.25	1.93	1.50	1.12	.90	.75	.56	.45	.37
Cheltenham Book Italic	4.52	3.88	3.40	3.02	2.72	2.47	2.26	1.94	1.51	1.13	.91	.79	.57	.45	.38
Cheltenham Bold	4.09	3.50	3.06	2.73	2.45	2.23	2.04	1.75	1.36	1.02	.82	.68	.51	.41	.34
Cheltenham Ultra	3.28	2.81	2.46	2.18	1.96	1.79	1.64	1.40	1.09	.82	.65	.55	.41	.33	.27
Clarendon Medium	3.56	2.86	2.67	2.38	2.13	1.94	1.78	1.43	1.19	.89	.71	.59	.45	.36	.30
Clarendon Bold	3.56	2.86	2.67	2.38	2.13	1.94	1.78	1.43	1.19	.89	.71	.59	.45	.36	.30
Commercial Script	4.72	4.05	3.54	3.15	2.84	2.58	2.36	2.02	1.57	1.18	.94	.78	.59	.47	.39
Copperplate Light	2.72	2.32	2.04	1.82	1.62	1.48	1.36	1.16	.91	.68	.54	.45	.34	.27	.23
Copperplate Heavy	2.72	2.32	2.04	1.82	1.62	1.48	1.36	1.16	.91	.68	.54	.45	.34	.27	.23
Coronet	7.80	6.68	5.85	5.20	4.68	4.25	3.90	3.34	2.60	1.95	1.56	1.30	.97	.78	.65
Dom Casual Medium	7.17	6.15	5.38	4.78	4.30	3.91	3.58	3.07	2.38	1.79	1.43	1.19	.90	.72	.60
Dom Casual Bold	7.17	6.15	5.38	4.78	4.30	3.91	3.58	3.08	2.39	1.79	1.43	1.19	.90	.72	.60
English Times Medium	4.46	3.82	3.35	2.97	2.68	2.43	2.23	1.91	1.48	1.11	.89	.74	.55	.44	.37
English Times Italic	4.46	3.82	3.35	2.97	2.68	2.43	2.23	1.91	1.48	1.11	.89	.74	.55	.44	.37
English Times Bold	4.46	3.82	3.35	2.97	2.68	2.43	2.23	1.91	1.48	1.11	.89	.74	.55	.44	.37
English Times Bold Italic	4.46	3.82	3.35	2.97	2.68	2.43	2.23	1.91	1.48	1.11	.89	.74	.55	.44	.37
Eras Light	4.72	4.04	3.54	3.14	2.83	2.57	2.36	2.02	1.57	1.18	.94	.79	.59	.47	.39
Eras Book	4.51	3.86	3.38	3.01	2.70	2.46	2.25	1.93	1.50	1.13	.90	.75	.56	.45	.38
Eras Medium	4.24	3.64	3.18	2.66	2.55	2.32	2.12	1.82	1.33	1.06	.85	.66	.53	.42	.33
Eras Demi	3.96	3.40	2.97	2.64	2.38	2.16	1.98	1.70	1.32	.99	.79	.66	.50	.40	.33
Eras Bold	3.64	3.12	2.73	2.43	2.19	1.99	1.82	1.56	1.21	.91	.73	.61	.46	.36	.30
Eras Ultra	3.41	2.92	2.55	2.27	2.04	1.86	1.70	1.46	1.13	.85	.68	.57	.43	.34	.28
Flemish Script	6.76	5.78	5.07	4.50	4.05	3.68	3.38	2.89	2.25	1.69	1.35	1.13	.84	.68	.56
Florentine Script	6.00	5.14	4.50	4.00	3.60	3.27	3.00	2.57	2.00	1.50	1.20	1.00	.75	.60	.50
Floridian Script	6.10	5.24	4.58	4.07	3.67	3.33	3.05	2.62	2.04	1.53	1.22	1.02	.76	.61	.51
French Script	7.52	6.44	5.64	5.00	4.51	4.10	3.76	3.22	2.50	1.88	1.50	1.25	.94	.75	.62
Friz Quadrata Medium	4.07	3.49	3.05	2.71	2.44	2.22	2.04	1.74	1.35	1.02	.81	.67	.51	.40	.33
Friz Quadrata Bold	4.07	3.49	3.05	2.71	2.44	2.22	2.04	1.74	1.35	1.02	.81	.67	.51	.40	.33

How to calculate CPP at negative letterspacing settings

Copyfitting is based on a calculation called "characters per pica." Most type books have this information listed for certain point sizes. They do not have it for every point size available, nor do they have it for each size at each possible white space reduction (negative letterspacing) value. Before we tell you how to *calculate* CPP (characters per pica) let us review how it is used for copyfitting.

1. Get a total of all the characters in your manuscript. Don't forget to count the word spaces.

2. Check the face and size and the line length that will be used. Look up the CPP and multiply it by the line length. If the CPP is 2.81 and the line length is 25 picas, the number 70.25 tells you how many characters will fit in one line.

3. Divide that number into the total number of characters and you will have the number of lines that the job will set.

4. Multiply the number of lines by your leading value to arrive at the copy depth (in points). If the job is mostly straight text you can figure the number of lines per page and divide to get the total number of pages. If there are many subheads, drop heads, illustrations, etc., you will have to estimate these separately.

Characters per pica information is used by designers and editors to see if their manuscript copy will fit in the space allocated. If not, they change the line length, point size—or go to a face with a greater CPP value or, in today's automated photocomposition market, they can ask for white space reduction values to tighten the copy up. When you call for WSR to take effect you change the listed CPP values. They are no longer valid.

To calculate the CPP for any point size you must first add up the lowercase alphabet in *units*. In an 18 unit system, each character has a width that is expressed in multiples of 18. The type specimen pages usually have this information or it may be on your font information sheet. Let's use 18 for an example.

Divide the total relative units in the lowercase alphabet (LCA) by 18 and multiply it by the point size. Divide the result into 342 and the answer is the CPP for that font in that size. If you use WSR, it is usually in ⅛th of a unit increments. So, just subtract .125 for each unit of WSR from the LCA before you start the equation. Do all calculations to two decimal points. You will find that the fineness of white space reduction does not have a significant effect until 4 or more units.

Here is a recap of the formula:

$$\frac{\textit{Number of relative units in lowercase alphabet}}{18} \times \textit{Point size} = \textit{Number of points}$$

$$\frac{342}{\textit{Number of points}} = \textit{Characters per pica}$$

Remember to subtract .125 from Relative Units for each unit of white space reduction.

Alternate Characters

Some typefaces have multiple versions of the same letter in the font to allow a greater variety of letter combinations. Specimen showings normally show all character variants with an identifying number for specification purposes.

Multiple versions of the same character are available to allow more creativity in headline setting. The key to their use is *restraint*—use as few as possible. Most alternate characters are "swash" versions that over- or under-hang adjacent characters.

A type character designed with certain characters having "flourished" beginnings or endings is called "swash."

"Bookman" was one of the first typefaces to have alternate characters. "Avant Garde" has both alternate characters and alternate combinations of characters.

A	B	C	D	E	F	G	H	I	J
A	B		D	E	F	G	H	I	J
K	L	M	N	O	P	Q	R	S	T
K	L	M	N		P		R	S	T
U	V	W	X	Y	Z	a	b	c	d
U	V	W	X	Y		a			
e	f	g	h	i	j	k	l	m	n
	f		h			k		m	n
o	p	q	r	s	t	u	v	w	x
				s	t				
y	z	1	2	3	4	5	6	7	8
9	0	$	.	,	:	;	" "	-	—
		$							
( )	*	?	!	&	¢	%	#	/	
[ ]									fi

a e b fgh k n pr t v w y
A ABCDEFGHHIJKK KLLMMNNOPQ
RRSTUVVWWXYYZ

FS Book Bold

A A ABBBCGDEEFGGHHIIJJJ
KKLLMMNNOOPPQQRRRSSTT
UUVVVWWWXXYYZZ&
abcdee fgh fi h fii jkKl mm n n oo ppqq
rr st t uvwxyz ß
$1234567890 ¹²³⁴⁵⁶⁷⁸⁹⁰ 1234567890 ¹²³⁴⁵⁶⁷⁸⁹⁰

Bookman italic

A A A B C C A C D E
E A F F A R G G A H H T
I J K I K A L L A L A L L M M
M N N T O P R Q R
R A S S S S T S T T H U U T
V V V W W V W X
Y Z & (",;"")?!(*)a b
c c d e e f ff fi fl ffi ffl
g h i j k l m n o p
q r s t t u v v v w w w
x y y z $ 1 2 3 4 5 6 7
8 9 0 ¢ / £ $ % #

Avant Garde Book

13

Ampersand

The ampersand (&) was originally a ligature (*et*, Latin for *and*) and repeated as part of the alphabet, at the end, as *"et per se, and"* (that is, et by itself, and) which became corrupted to "and per se and." In some ampersand designs, the e and t are distinguishable. A small cap ampersand often works better than the usual cap version, especially when used with lowercase letters. Used in titles and company names primarily.

Apex

This is the top junction to two stems and is most often evident in the point of the cap A and the center of the cap W. The opposite of an apex—that is the bottom junction of two stems—is the *vortex*. Our cap W has one apex and two vortex points:

The inside of an apex or vortex is a "crotch."

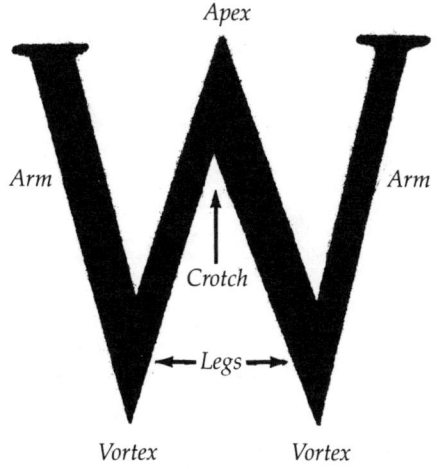

Arrows

Available in many pi fonts, in open or closed versions, pointing in most directions, usually left, right, up and down, or combinations. Here are some:

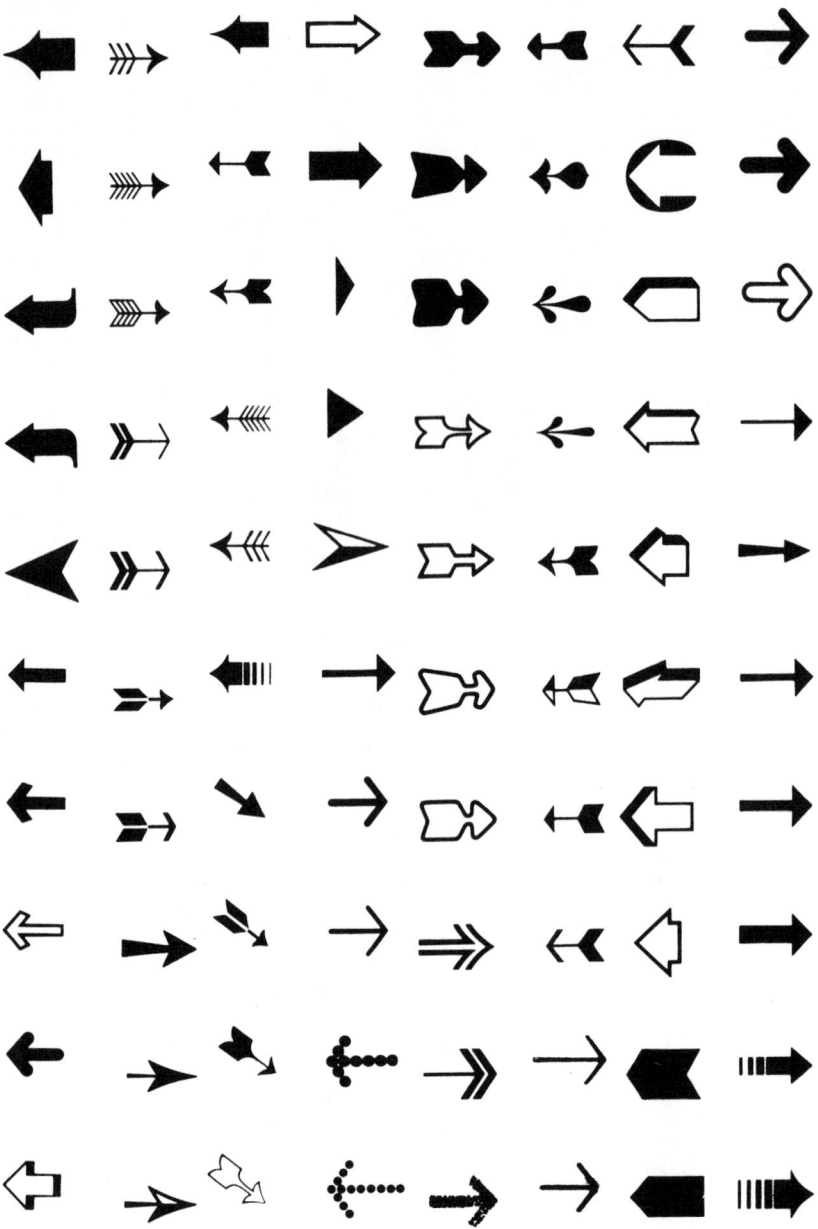

16

Ascender

Ascending characters are the b d f h k l t. They rise above the x-height and may not always align (although most do) at the top.

One must be careful that line spacing or leading is sufficient so that the ascenders of one line do not touch the descenders of another line.

In Old Roman typefaces the ascenders are taller than the caps.

The descending characters are g j p q y. They descend below the x-height and usually align at the bottom.

Typefaces are designed with descenders to meet the designer's creative feeling—thus some may be shorter (or longer) than others.

Ascender line

bdfhklt

Ascending characters

Not all ascenders align

b d f h k l t

Descending characters

g j p q y

Long vs. short descenders

Actually just one point

Long or short descenders are the province of the typeface designer

b

Biform

Blackletter

Book Typography

Borders

Boxes and Bullets

Bracketed

Brush

Biform

Refers to the intermingling of modified small cap and lowercase characters in the formation of a lowercase alphabet. Type set with such characters has a unique appearance. The most famous biform face is "Peignot."

Biforms are most often used in heads or subheads or advertising display; rarely in text unless you're an 11th century scribe.

Biforms are derived from the uncial versions of handwritten styles. See **Uncial**.

AbcdefGhijklMNopQRstuvwxyz
ABCDEFGHIJKLMNOPQRSTUVWXYZ
1234567890 1234567890 (&.,:;!?"-*$¢%/£)

Peignot Light

AbcdefGhijklMNopQRstuvwxyz
ABCDEFGHIJKLMNOPQRSTUVWXYZ
1234567890 1234567890 [&.,:;!?''""-*$¢%/£]

Peignot Demibold

AbcdefGhijklMNopQRstuvwxyz
ABCDEFGHIJKLMNOPQRSTUVWXYZ
1234567890 1234567890 (&.,:;!?''""-*$¢%/£)

Peignot Bold

Blackletter

This includes the typefaces derived from the German writing hand of the 13th century. Sometimes called "Textura" since it appeared to "weave a texture" on the page. Blackletter typefaces were used in Germany until the 1930s.

Also called Spire-Gothic, "Old English," as well as Blackletter. (In the past, Americans also used the word gothic as a synonym for sans serif.)

This Style of Black-letter resembles that used by Johann Gutenberg for his Bible of Forty-two Lines. William Caxton, who began as a printer with types now known as Old Flemish, afterward made use of this earlier form, as then cut and cast by the type-founders of France. As this form has been used in England for more than three hundred years for the Official Copies of all Acts of Parliament, for the Book of Common Prayer, and Ecclesiastical Forms, it has fairly earned the name of OLD ENGLISH. Bookish men agree in rating this as the Standard form of Black-letter.

THIS HELYAS TYPE is a faithful reproduction of the type used by Wynkyn de Worde in his edition of Helyas or Knight of the Swanne, dated London, 1513. Re printed from the unique copy of Mr. Robert Hoe, by the Grolier Club of the City of New York. It was cast in the type-foundry of Sir Charles Reed's Sons of London, who are the owners of the surviving punches and matrices of the Star Chamber founders and their predecessors. This face and that of the Philobiblon letter are preferred by all book lovers for the reprinting of Old English texts, in books of compact or convenient form.

THIS HELYAS TYPE

This Style of Type was designed for the reprinting of medieval books or subject matter, but it has been and is now freely used for modern books, and even for mercantile advertisements and circulars. Its lower-case letters are fairly readable, but some of its capitals are extremely uncouth and cannot be made pleasing in any combinations. Lines of capitals that contain the characters F J L T W and Y are usually rejected in the proof.

abcdefghijklmnopqrsftu
ABCDEFGHIJKLM
UVWXYZ 123456789

Book Typography

The arrangement of the various parts of a book is relatively standardized by custom, even though some of the parts may be missing.

Front Matter

Half Title: Book title alone on page.

Fact Title: List of books by same author (faces Title Page).

Title Page: Always a right hand (recto) page.

Copyright: Must be on Title Page or, commonly, on the reverse.

Dedication: May be on Copyright page, usually a recto page.

Preface: (Foreword, Introduction)

Acknowledgment

Table of Contents: Always recto.

List of Illustrations

List of Figures: Maps, Charts, Tables

Introduction: Always recto.

Text

Back Matter

Appendix: Notes, Quotations, Bibliography, Glossary

Index

Colophon: Provides production details.

Front Matter pages are numbered with Roman numerals, i thru xviii, for example, in lowercase.

The following terms refer to the setting of pages for books.

Verso, the left page.

Recto, the right page.

Folio, the page number.

Running head, or *Running foot,* the book name (usualy) appearing on every page, top or bottom.

Chapter opening, the first page of a chapter, usualy a recto page.

Line short/Line long, the allowance for setting certain pages one line longer or shorter than page depth to eliminate widows or short pages, or make allowance for illustrations or tables.

Widow, the last line of a paragraph less than one third the width of the line, usually the carryover of a hyphenated word.

Orphan, a widow carried to the top of the next page.

A sheet of paper printed as one page is a *broadside*.
Fold it once and it is a *folio* (4 pages)
Fold it twice and it is a *quarto* (8 pages)
Fold it three times and it is a *octavo* (16 pages)
Fold it four times and it is a *16 mo* (32 pages)
Fold it five times and it is a *32 mo* (64 pages)

The first colophon appeared in Fust and Schoeffer's Psalter of 1457. The colophon describes certain production information about the book, most often about the typography.

Borders

A border is a frame that can be placed around type, graphic, pictorial or other material. A border should complement or harmonize with the material it surrounds. The most important consideration involves corners that meet properly.

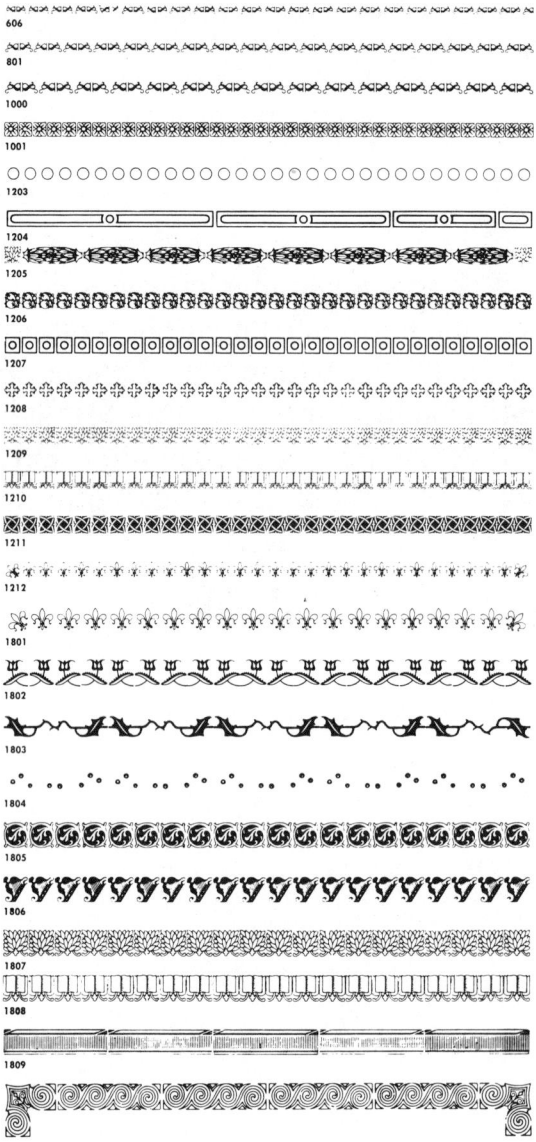

Boxes and Bullets

The two most common non-character characters used in typography are boxes and bullets:

Boxes (or Squares) □ (Open) ■ (Closed)

Bullets ○ (Open) ● (Closed)

They should be as close to the x-height as possible if used full size, or centered on it if not. More often than not you will have to change point size so that the box or bullet will optically match the x-height.

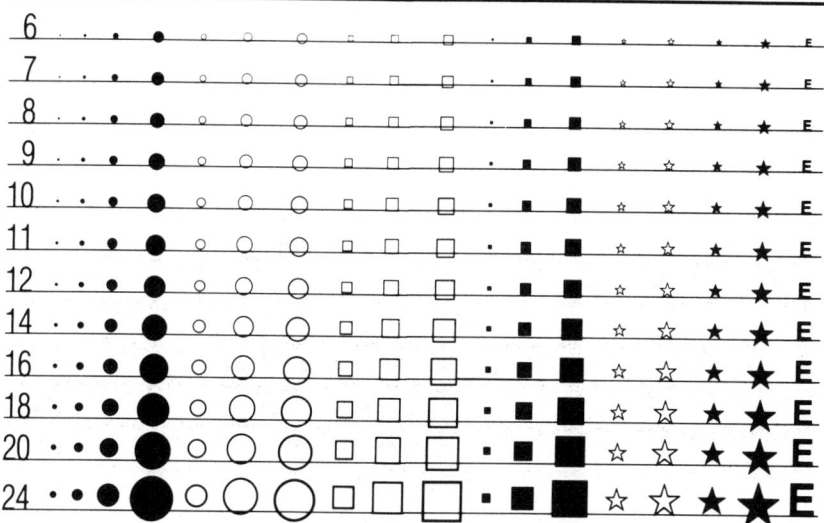

Courtesy: Expertype

Bracketed

This term describes the linking of the main stem of a character (vertical) to the serif (horizontal). Bracketing may be "fine" or "full" depending upon the amount of attachment.

A square serif typeface is called an "Egyptian," but when it is bracketed it is a "Clarendon." Most "Old Roman" style and "Transitional" romans are bracketed, but "Modern" romans are not.

"Egyptian" typefaces derive their name (Cairo, Memphis, Karnak, etc.) from the Egyptian campaign of Napoleon, who supposedly used these very readable characters on large sign boards for telescope viewing and thus long distance message relay. They are also called "square" or "slab" serifs.

Bracketed

Unbracketed

An "Egyptian"

Brush

Typefaces which appear to have been drawn with a brush or broad pointed pen. A casual or informal feeling results from the use of "brush" faces.

Used in greeting cards and special purpose promtions. Sometimes used to simulate a handwritten message, but a more formal "script" may be more appropriate.

abcdefghijklmnopqrstuvwxyz
ABCDEFGHIJKLMNOPQRSTUVWXYZ
1234567890 (&.,:; ""…!?-$¢%/)*

Brush

Brush American

Champion

C

Calligraphy

Capitals

Cap Line

Closed

Color, Typographic

Condensed

Contour

Contrast

Copperplate

Counter

Cyrillic

Calligraphy

Calligraphy is "beautiful writing" and also a form of *lettering*, which is the drawing of letters by hand. Typography is lettering adapted and made more orderly for special purposes, such as a mechanical reproduction.

The "Chancery" script of the 15th Century became the model for our *italics*, and the writing masters of the period—Palatino, for one—developed techniques for formal handwriting.

A calligraphic typeface based on the Renaissance "Chancery" hand

Contemporary calligraphy by Arthur Baker

Capitals

The letters A through Z, usually including the ampersand. All-cap words or acroynyms in text should be small caps. In heads, they are usually set as caps with minimum word spacing and, optionally, letterspaced slightly.

The space between words should not be greater than the space between lines. Mechanical line-up of caps on the left usually results in uneven alignment:

Left Alignment **Now You Can Tell**   **Now You Can Tell** *Optical Alignment*

Optical or visual alignment requires some kerning to achieve better looking line-up, as illustrated in this sample.

Since many of us are accustomed to thinking of sizes in terms of point size, we have tried to relate this to cap height. This table is based on Franklin Gothic whose caps range from approximately 66% to not more than 83% of body size.

Point Size in Points	*Minimum Cap Height*
12	8
14	9⅓
16	10⅔
18	12
20	13½
24	16
30	20
36	24
42	29
48	32
54	39
60	40
72	48
84	57¾
96	67½
108	72¼
120	81

Cap Line

An imaginary line defining the height of the capital letters of a particular typeface. Caps can be higher or lower than ascending characters. Old (Roman) Style typefaces usually have caps shorter than the ascenders.

Ascender may or may not align with cap line.

Cap Line **Plug** *x-height*

Closed

A character or symbol that is essentially "filled in" or solid; the opposite of *open*, which describes a character of symbol that exists as an outline.

★ ★ ☆ ☆
Closed   *Open*

In the use of dashes, closed refers to the absence of space on either end of the dash; open means that there is a space.

Word — Word
Open

Word—Word
Closed

We preferred open dash usage to allow the typesetter, or system, more places to end lines. Since a word space might be too wide and a fixed space (a thin, perhaps) might make the combination unacceptable for line termination, we suggested you kern the word space to half of its optimum value. This last suggestion does not apply to sophisticated computer typesetting systems.

Color, Typographic

The "color" of your page of type refers to the overall shade of gray perceived by your eye, which might be interrupted by bad word or character spacing or uneven leading. "Typographic" color can only be accomplished by reviewing type after setting.

Rivers are patterns of white that result from the random position of word spaces in adjacent lines. Again, you must review type after setting to find and correct problems with "typographic color."

These areas should be watched:

1. Word spacing (keep consistent)
2. Widowed lines (reduce where possible)
3. Poor letter spacing (kerning needed)
4. Uneven right margin caused by too many hyphens in a row (re-set)
5. A general, even, consistent appearance (including the density or "blackness" of the type).

Condensed

Refers to the narrowness of all characters in one type style. Condensed typefaces are used where large amounts of copy must fit into a relatively small space; tabular composition being the most common area of usage. This is a variation in width.

There are even gradations of condensation: ultra-condensed, extra-condensed, condensed, semi-condensed. The words "narrow" and "compressed" are sometimes used as a synonym for these levels of condensing.

Digitized typesetters, in many cases, can "condense" characters by defining new set widths. Thus, 12-point characters can be specified as 11½ set—unlike hot metal and early phototypesetters, which merely removed space on sides of characters, but retained their width. The digitized devices acutally make the character narrower, electronically.

Of course, there are differences in characters condensed by a type designer in designing the face and characters condensed optically (by lenses) or digitally by machines. These are not usually apparent to the uneducated eye, and thus more typeface variations—condensing and expanding—are machine-created.

Optical Condensing

Normal — **With the use of s**

Condensed — 8% **With the use of sp**

16% **With the use of spe**

24% **With the use of spe**

34% **With the use of spec**

Remember, a condensed typeface still has an EM space that is a square formed by the value of the point size. Thus, fixed widths will appear wider than normal. If you "condense" a typeface by changing the set width, then all values will change, even the fixed spaces.

Contour

Setting type in a "shape," therefore creating the appearance of an object, is called a contour or run-around. It is accomplished via multiple line indents. A special sheet with pica and point gradations is used to calculate the value of the indents.

The sheet is usually transparent and placed over the art or shape so that all indents can be established.

Been reached regarding its use in management accounting. Discounting has been applied in isolated instances (e.g., to account for certain leases, pension plans, and long-term receivables and payables), but its overall relevance to financial accounting has not been clarified. The Accounting Principles Board (APB) recognized, in 1966 and 1967, the need for reaching conclusions concerning the broader aspects of discounting as it is related to financial accounting in general.
Even with the APB action, a void remains which is explained, in part, by the absence of stated objectives of financial statements that are necessary for defining the conceptual foundations of financial accounting. Agreement on the objectives of financial statements is essential for determining how accounting data should be measured and classified and for specifying the qualitative characteristics that accounting information should possess. The time value of money is an important attribute of some assets and liabilities. Measurement of this attribute should provide meaningful information for users of financial statements irrespective of the approach to valuation deemed appropriate in a conceptual framework for financial accounting and reporting. That is, the applicability of discounting as one dimensions of measurement is independent of whether accounting is based on historical costs or current values. Board, APB Opinion No. 10, "Omnibus Opinion—1966," December, 1966, paragraph 6, and APB Opinion No. 11, "Accounting for Income Taxes," December, 1967, paragraph 3.

This study, which consists of three parts, is responsive to the APB's suggestion, more than a decade ago, that research is needed for determining the role of discounting in financial accounting. Part I attempts to accomplish the following:
Present value theory is well established in economics, finance, and actuarial science, and general agreement has been reached regarding its use in management accounting. Discounting has been applied in isolated instances (e.g., to account for certain leases, pension plans, and long-term receivables and payables), but its overall relevance to financial accounting has not been clarified. The Accounting Principles Board (APB) recognized, in 1966 and 1967, the need for reaching conclusions concerning the broader aspects of discounting as it is related to financial accounting in general.
Even with the APB action, a void remains which is explained, in part, by the absence of stated objectives of financial statements that are necessary for defining the conceptual foundations of financial accounting. Agreement on the objectives of financial statements is essential for determining how accounting data should be measured and classified and for specifying the qualitative characteristics that accounting information should possess. The time value of money is an important attribute of some assets and liabilities. Measurement of this attribute should provide meaningful information for users of financial statements irrespective of the approach to valuation deemed appropriate in a conceptual framework for financial accounting and reporting.

"Negative" contours

Present value theory is well established in economics, finance, and actuarial science, and general agreement has been reached regarding its use in management accounting. Discounting has been applied in isolated instances (e.g., to account for certain leases, pension plans, and long-term receivables and payables), but its overall relevance to financial accounting has not been clarified. The Accounting Principles Board (APB) recognized, in 1966 and 1967, the need for reaching conclusions concerning the broader aspects of discounting as it is related to financial accounting in general.
Even with the APB action, a void remains which is explained, in part, by the absence of stated objectives of financial statements that are necessary for defining the conceptual foundations of financial accounting. Agreement on the objectives of financial statements is essential for determining how accounting data should be measured and classified and for specifying the qualitative characteristics that accounting information should possess. The time value of money is an important attribute of some assets and liabilities. Measurement of this attribute should provide meaningful information for users of 9nancial statements irrespective of the approach to valuation deemed appropriate in a conceptual framework for financial accounting and reporting. That is, the applicability of discounting as one dimensidons of measurement is independent of whether accounting is based on historical costs or current values.
Board, APB Opinion No. 10, "Omnibus Opinion—1966," December, 1966, paragraph 6, and APB Opinion No. 11, "Accounting for Income Taxes," December, 1967, paragraph 3.
This study, which consists of three parts, is responsive to the APB's suggestion, more than a decade ago, that research is needed for determining the role of discounting in financial accounting. Part I attempts to accomplish the following:

Present value theory is well established in economics, finance, and actuarial science, and general agreement has been reached regarding its use in management accounting. Discounting has been applied in isolated instances (e.g., to account for certain leases, pension plans, and long-term receivables and payables), but its overall relevance to financial accounting has not been clarified. The Accounting Principles Board (APB) recognized, in 1966 and 1967, the need for reaching conclusions concerning the broader aspects of discounting as it is related to financial accounting in general.
Even with the APB action, a void remains which is explained, in part, by the absence of stated objectives of financial statements that are necessary for defining the conceptual foundations of financial accounting. Agreement on the objectives of financial statements is essential for determining how accounting data should be measured and classified and for specifying the qualitative characteristics that accounting information should possess. The time value of money is an important attribute of some assets and liabilities. Measurement of this attribute should provide meaningful information for users of financial statements irrespective of the approach to valuation deemed appropriate in a conceptual framework for financial accounting and reporting. That is, the applicability of discounting as one dimensidons of measurement is independent of whether accounting is based on historical costs or current values.
Board, APB Opinion No. 10, "Omnibus Opinion—1966," December, 1966, paragraph 6, and APB Opinion No. 11, "Accounting for Income Taxes," December, 1967, paragraph 3.
This study, which consists of three parts, is responsive to the APB's suggestion, more than a decade ago, that research is needed for determining the role of discounting in financial accounting. Part I attempts to accomplish the following:

"Positive" contours

At the National Safety Council Honors Drunk Driving Efforts of Non Governmental gro psthe National Safety Council has announced a new program of financial grants and recognition to non-governmental organizations and individuals who are conducting programs to curb the drinking driver menace. The grants to organizations, individuals, and institutions are funded by General Motors Foundation, Inc., and the Mobil Foundation, Inc. The Council is setting up a panel to consider entries for the grant program, with the following criteria: action must be directly related to the drinking driver problem; proat a driver menace. The grants to organizations, individuals, and institutions are funded by General Motors Foundation, Inc., and the Mobil Foundation, Inc. The Council is setting up a panel to consider entries to the nation

CONTOUR LEADING LAYOUT CHART
13 Point Leading

Sold Only By:
Tom Lubeck
P.O. Box 509
Berwyn, IL 60402

37

Contrast

Essentially, a **difference** between items. In typography, we deal with contrasts in:

1. Size
2. Weight
3. Width
4. Form
5. Structure
6. Placement
7. Posture

. . . and combinations of them.

BIG SMALL
BOLD LIGHT
WIDE NARROW
SANS SERIF

Copperplate

A type style created out of necessity in the days of copperplate engraving (an older form of printing) which has fine serifs at the ends of all strokes.

Instead of pens or brushes, copperplate engraving was done on a fine polished copper plate with a steel scribe.

In order to get good sharp corners on the strokes, a final scribe was made perpendicular to the main stroke and was allowed to extend just a bit beyond, creating the copperplate serifs. After printing, or in small point sizes, Copperplate serifs often became indistinguishable.

Copperplate typefaces do not usually have a lowercase, using smaller point size caps in place of them. Used primarily for business cards or business stationery, Copperplate should *never* be used for text paragraphs.

COPPERPLATE SERIES
ABCDEFGHIJKLMNOPQRSTUVWXYZ
& — 1234567890$

ABCDEFGHIJKLMNOPQRSTUVWXYZ& — 1234567890$
( ) 0 [] [] // %% *_- .. :: !? - ¨

Counter

Refers to the fully or partially enclosed part of a letter as in the lowercase *e,FP* which has a full counter above and a partial below. Counter refers to the *space*, where the term "bowl" refers to the lines enclosing the counter.

   A "complete" bowl is formed by curved strokes only, and a "modified" bowl has the stem forming one of the sides. A "loop" is a bowl that serves as a florish, as the decending part of some lowercase g characters.

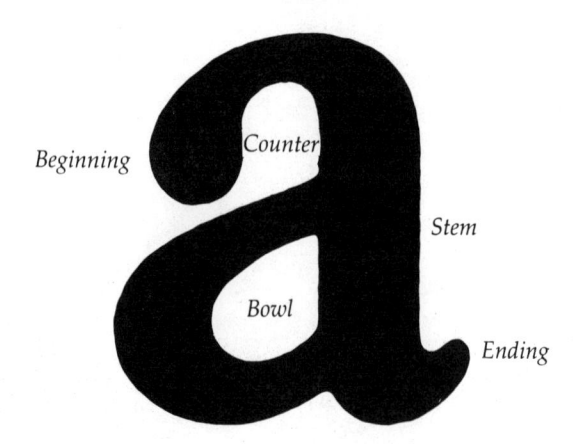

Cyrillic

Saint Cyril brought learning to Eastern Europe by establishing monasteries and learning, and the alphabet that evolved included unique characters and accents—and combinations of them. Cyrillic refers to language and alphabets common to Russia, Czechoslovakia, Yugoslavia and Turkey.

АБВГДЕЁЖЗИЙКЛМНОПРСТУФХЦЧ
ЫЬЭЮЯабвгдеёжзийклмнопрстуфх
ъыьэюя 1234567890(.,:;!?«»

The above typeface is a cyrillic version of Helvetica.

d

Dashes

Digitized Typography

Dashes

Ranging from the smallest to the largest, here are the dashes that are used in typography:

Hyphen

The hyphen is used for breaking words on syllables at the end of lines to allow even spacing in justification and for compound or connected words (*mother-in-law*).

En Dash

The en dash is used where the word "to" or "through" is represented, such as "Pages 1–9" or "January 13–19." It also connects two nouns of equal weight, such as "East–West" alliance. The en dash may also replace a colon. If you do not have an en dash, kern two hyphens together. The en dash should always be closed (no space on either side).

¾ Em Dash

This is just a slightly smaller em dash and is used where the em dash itself appears too wide for the typeface in use.

Em Dash

The em dash (and ¾ em) are used to indicate missing material such as "Dr. — was the murderer" or for parenthetical remarks to show a break in thought or special emphasis, such as "Hello—he thought at the time—." Em dashes are also used to replace a colon, "Here's the list—"

Em dashes may be open — with a word space on either side of it — or closed—with no space. The open style allows for more alternatives for end-of-line breaks although some newer systems will break at an em dash if it occurs at the end of a line.

Dashes should not be carried over to the beginning of the following line, if possible.

Rule Line

The rule line (often, but not always, aligning at the baseline) is used for horizontal ruling, including underlining.

The problem with a line of rules is that the width of the rule may not divide evenly into the line length. Rules are commonly the EM width, the width of the point size. If the line length is an even number of picas, the 12 point rule (12 pts. wide) would go in evenly. If the line length is in half picas the 6 point rule (6 pts. wide) would divide enenly. If there is other copy on the line, then there is only luck. Since the typesetting machine might put the excess space at the end, you should put a word space between the other copy and the start of the rule so the excess space has a place to go. This may not be so with newer digitized typesetters.

HAIRLINE RULE

ONE-HALF POINT RULE

▬▬▬▬▬▬▬▬▬▬▬▬▬▬▬▬▬▬▬▬

THREE POINT RULE

▬▬▬▬▬▬▬▬▬▬▬▬▬▬▬▬▬▬▬▬

SIX POINT RULE

▬▬▬▬▬▬▬▬▬▬▬▬▬▬▬▬▬▬▬▬

EIGHT POINT RULE

- - - - - - - - - - - - - - - - - -

HAIRLINE LONG COUPON RULE

- -

ONE-HALF POINT SHORT COUPON RULE

─ ─ ─ ─ ─ ─ ─ ─ ─ ─ ─ ─ ─ ─ ─ ─

ONE-HALF POINT LONG COUPON RULE

■■ ■■ ■■ ■■ ■■ ■■ ■■ ■■ ■■

TWO POINT LONG COUPON RULE

██ ██ ██ ██ ██ ██ ██ ██ █

SIX POINT LONG COUPON RULE

Each point size creates a different weight for the dash.

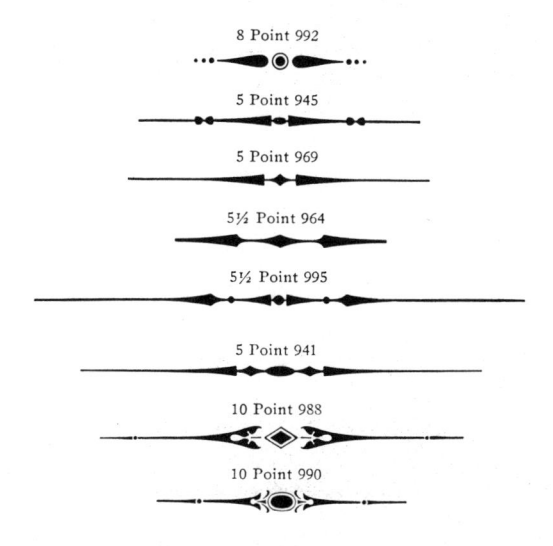

8 Point 992

5 Point 945

5 Point 969

5½ Point 964

5½ Point 995

5 Point 941

10 Point 988

10 Point 990

Ornamental dashes (also called "Bodoni" dashes).

Digitized Typography

Digital type gets its name from digital computers, which are based on the binary principle of ON/OFF. A digital image is created with dots and the individual dot is either there or not there—on or off.

The individual dot is also called a *pel* or *pixel* (both terms are shorthand for "picture element") and a group of overlapping dots forming a straight or curved line is called a *raster*.

Typesetters that use line segments or "vectors" to outline a character still use dots as the basic building blocks.

All digital typesetters (sometimes called "third generation" devices) use the very basic principle of turning some light source on and off to create an image. That light source can be a cathode ray tube (CRT) or a laser or it may not be a light source at all as newer technologies apply elecro erosion, magnetography and light emitting diodes.

The placement of the dots for an individual character is stored in memory. Rather than turn the imaging source on and off for each dot, many devices employ a principle called "run-length of coding" which allows the beam to sweep continuously over a series of ON dots rather than turning on and off for each one.

Because every character is made up of dots, diagonals and curves may not be as smooth and sharp in their edge resolution as straight lines. At 1,000 dots per inch, a measurement of resolution, acceptable quality is produced. At 5,000 lines per inch, there is no visible difference between digital type and other photographic type.

The best place to check quality levels is the dot on the lowercase i or the entire typeface Optima.

Since digital type exists in memory or "program" form, it may be manipulated electronically to produce:

1. More point size increments. Some units use ⅒ of a point increments.
2. Oblique or backslant characters. Permissible for use in sans serifs only.
3. Expanded or condensed characters.
4. Reverse images.

In time all typesetting and image generation will be digital.

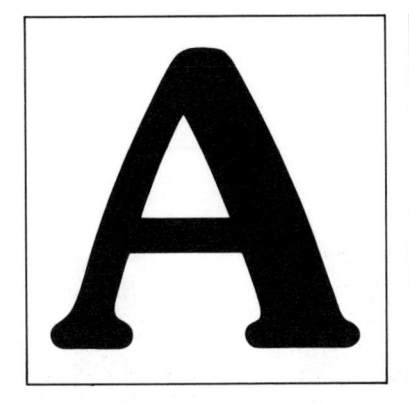

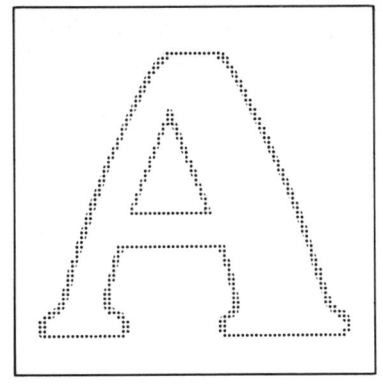

12° slant

hello

Reverse

hello

12° slant reverse

hello

Condensed

hello

Expanded

hello

(Above) Digitized characters are made up of individual dots, overlapped to form lines (rasters) and turned on and off to create either a character outline (which is then "painted" in with dots) or the actual character directly. At left, you can see some of the electronic modifications that are possible.

             A   B   C

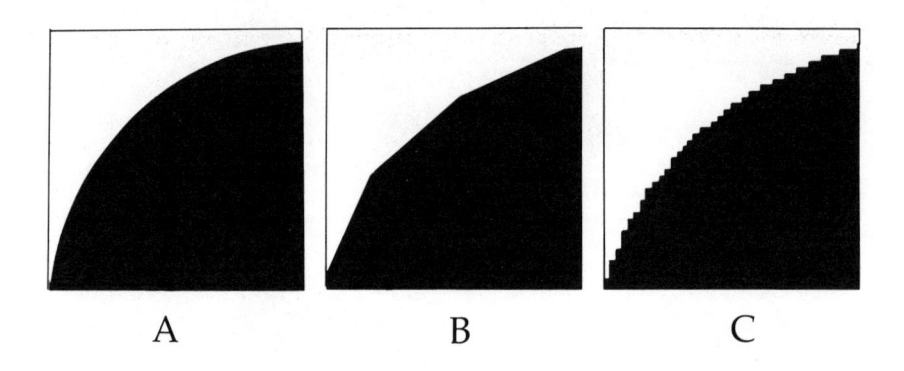

The edge gradient tells the tale in terms of digital quality. Vector devices (B) use larger line segments (which sort of "connect the dots" of the character outline), while pure raster devices (C) create a swatooth effect. There is no technical reason why you could not have a clean edge as in "A." Most of these "problems" are not visible to the unaided eye.

e

Ellipses

Emphasis

Expanded

Ellipses

Better known as the "three periods" that indicate that something is missing (omission) or that conversation has stopped (interruption). If a sentence is complete, the period is set close, followed by the three points:

"The end is near. . . . or, at least, close."

The problem with these darned dots is that they may fall at the end of a line, and then several things can happen.

1. If you spaced them with thin spaces, the machine may see them as one unit and not break them, thus forcing a tight line or necessitating a badly spaced one.

2. If you used word spaces between the points, you will have eratic spacing—too wide or too close—based on the justification requirements of the line. The word space will help if they fall at the end of the line. An alternative is to use "kerned word spaces."

3. You could space the dots with thin spaces but insert a word space (kerned) between them and the preceding word.

4. Or, you could use "kerned word spaces" between the periods.

And, fortunately, some computer typesetting systems handle them automatically.

Emphasis

Typography provides more opportunities for emphasizing information than typewriters or line printers:

    ALL CAPITALS
    SMALL CAPITALS
    CAPS & SMALL CAPS
    Underlined
    Italic
    ITALIC CAPS
    ITALIC CAPS & SMALL CAPS
    ITALIC SMALL CAPS
    Bold
    BOLD CAPS
    BOLD CAPS & SMALL CAPS
    BOLD SMALL CAPS
    Bold Italic
    ITALIC BOLD CAPS
    ITALIC BOLD CAPS & SMALL CAPS
    ITALIC BOLD SMALL CAPS

Expanded

Usually refers to the width or wideness of all characters in a particular type style. Expanded faces are often used for heads, sub-heads and small blocks of ad copy. This is a variation in width.

There are gradations—semi-expanded, expanded, extra-expanded and ultra-expanded. These are subjective terms. The terms "extended" and "wide" are often used as synonyms. Note that "Century Expanded," for example, is expanded in the "x-height" direction, not in its width.

Digitized typesetters can modify character "set width" electronically to create wider characters. Expansion can also be accomplished optically.

Of course, you would not use expanded typefaces with narrow line lengths (but you already know that).

Optical expansion

Expanded — **With the use**
8%
With the use
16%
With the use
24%
With the us
34%

The fixed spaces (EM space, for example) are based on the point size and may be smaller than required for an expanded face. However, if a digitized typesetter was used to reduce set size, then all values were changed, including the fixed spaces.

CENTURY EXPANDED

THIS face of type was first made on 10-point body, for use on THE CENTURY MAGAZINE, and it has been used for many books of The Century Co. The expansion of the letter is upward, enabling one to get much matter in small space.

Century Expanded is not really expanded—it has a larger x-height or "upward expansion" as DeVinne said.

f

Figures
Fixed Space
Font
Footnotes and References
Format
Fractions

Figures

The 1 through 0 come in two versions:

Old Style or Old Face (or Non-aligning)

Lining (or Modern)

In text, numbers under 100 should be spelled out unless they relate to specific references. Always spell out at the beginning of a sentence.

All figures must be the same width to allow tabular lineup when in tabs or listing; this does not apply to dates.

1 2 3 4 5 6 7 8 9 0   *Lining numerals (modern)*

1 2 3 4 5 6 7 8 9 0   *Non-aligning numerals (old style)*

1	I	40	XL	500	D
2	II	41	XLI	600	DC
4	IV	49	IL	900	CM
5	V	50	L	1000	M
6	VI	60	LX	1981	MCMLXXXI
7	VII	90	XC	2000	MM
9	IX	100	C	5000	V̄
10	X	101	CI	10,000	X̄
11	XI	150	CL	100,000	C̄
20	XX	200	CC	1,000,000	M̄
30	XXX	400	CD		

Roman numerals

① ② ③ ④ ⑤ ⑥ ⑦ ⑧ ⑨ ⑩
❶ ❷ ❸ ❹ ❺ ❻ ❼ ❽ ❾ ❿
① ② ③ ④ ⑤ ⑥ ⑦ ⑧ ⑨ ⑩
❶ ❷ ❸ ❹ ❺ ❻ ❼ ❽ ❾ ❿
1 2 3 4 5 6 7 8 9 10
1 2 3 4 5 6 7 8 9 10
① ② ③ ④ ⑤ ⑥ ⑦ ⑧ ⑨ ⑩
1 2 3 4 5 6 7 8 9 10

Multiple digit numerals can be created within oblongs using sorts as shown.

Fixed Space

Where a constant-width blank space is required, you use spaces of certain fixed increments, since typographic *word* spaces vary in width according to the justification needs of a line.

The most common widths are the EM (a square formed by the valve of the point size—a 9-point EM space will be 9-points wide no matter what the face), the EN (half the EM) and the THIN (either ¼ or ⅓ of an EM). The FIGURE space would have the same width as the numerals 1–10 and the dollar sign, although the EN may be used for this in some systems.

If you require fixed spaces of a certain number of points, remember that the EM is as wide as the point size. If you need two picas of horizontal space, set 2 EMs in 12-point (1 pica = 12-points).

The EM is also the maximum relative unit value, so, in a 54 unit system, the EM is 54 units . . . and so for 18 and 36 unit systems.

In most type families the EM space is designed as a square of the point size, i.e., for 12-point type the EM space would be 12-points high by 12-points wide. The EN space would be proportionately half as wide as the EM and the THIN space one-third or one-quarter of the width of the EM. Variations would occur when the type is condensed or expanded. In these cases, while always being the same height as the point size, the widths of the fixed spaces might vary according to the style of the type.

Whether the EM space is a square of the point size or not, the value would be 54 units. An increase in point size, while increasing the size of the fixed spaces, also increases proportionately the size of the units. Therefore, units are relative, the larger the point size being used, the larger each of the units will be, but the **number** of units will not change.

Remember, an EM has no value until you select the point size. A "10 EM indent" in 9-point is different from one in 11-point.

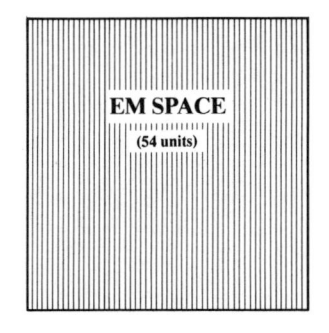

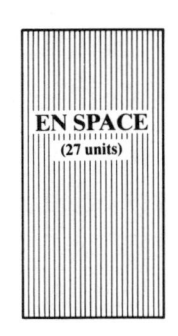

| EM SPACE (54 units) | EN SPACE (27 units) | THIN SPACE (18 units) |

36-pt.
EM
36 points wide

60-pt.
EM
60 points wide

72-pt.
EM
72 points wide

36-pt.
EN
18 points wide

60-pt.
EN
30 points wide

72-pt.
EN
36 points wide

Font

A font is a set of characters in a particular typeface (and point size in hot metal).

The term "wrong font" or "w.f." refers to an incorrect character—one that does not belong to the font.

A type font contains *all* of the alphanumerics, (letters, numbers) punctuation marks, special characters, ligatures, etc. contained in *ONE given version* of a typeface. An alphanumeric is any letter or numeral.

Purchasing the same font from two different sources may yield the addition or deletion of certain special characters:

1. One version may provide a % and ¢ while the other may provide an asterisk or bullet.

2. Another version may provide all of these things.

3. There might also be differences in design, weight and even point size.

Thus, the character complement, or font, may be completely contained, or may be used with a variety of pi fonts.

Also, in mark-up it is important to specify a font by its full and correct name: Helvetica Extra Bold Extended or Helv. X-Bold Ext. to prevent wasted time in typsetting in the wrong font.

ABCDEFGHIJKLMNOPQRSTU VWXYZ ˇˆ¨˜¯˙˚ ¸ÆŒØ (&.,:;'""!¡?¿.—-«»*)   *A typesetting font*

ABCDEFGHIJKLMNOPQRSTUVWXYZ&
abcdefghijklmnopqrstuvwxyz
1234567890$ ().,:;'"!? - _
½¼¾ % ¢ + = @ #

A typewriter font

Gutenberg's font

Footnotes and References

Marginal, parenthetical or reference material relating to the main body of text positioned at the bottom of the page. Footnotes are referenced by certain symbols (*, †, ‡, etc.), letters or numbers, most often in a superior form.

A footnote must begin on the same page as its "reference call" but may be carried over to the bottom of successive pages. A short rule or additional space separates the footnote from the text. Footnotes may also be placed at the end of its associated text. When used at this point they may also be called "references."

Point sizes for footnotes are most often 7-point or 8-point. By law, footnotes in financial forms, annual reports, prospectuses, and other SEC documents must be no smaller than the text size, which is 10-point.

The sequence of footnote references marks is:

Asterisk   *
(Single) Dagger   †
Double Dagger   ‡
Paragraph Symbol   ¶
Section Mark   §
Double Vertical Rule   ‖

. . . and if you still need more, double up: Double asterisks, double (single) daggers, double double daggers, etc.

Format

A format is any combination of point size, line spacing (leading), line length, typeface, placement and style that contribute to producing a specific typographic appearance. This may relate to a character, word, line, paragraph, section, page, group of pages, or an entire publication.

Formats can be expressed by indicating each of the items above or by using a shorthand approach: storing the format items and referencing them as a number, letter, or group of numbers and letters, depending on the system used.

For example:

[sf1] [cc 30, 10, 11, 1] [rr [ah [xl [ef]

This says Store Format 1 *Line Length* 30 picas
> *Point Size* 10
> *Line Spacing* (Leading) 11
> *Font* 1
> *Ragged Right*
> *Allow Hyphenation*
> *Cancel Letterspacing*

To use this format, you key:

[uf1]

And mark it up: 1

A format might detail all or most of the following:

1. Point size
2. Typeface
3. Line length
4. Leading
5. Justified or ragged
6. Letterspace requirements
7. Word space values
8. Indention requirements.

Fractions

Someday, the metric system may negate all this, but here are the forms of fractions:

EM Fractions

This is the most common form, each fraction on the EM width, with a diagonal stroke. Most devices have the ¼, ½, ¾ as standard.

EN Fractions

These are, of course, on the EN width and have a horizontal stroke, and are used when a vast number of odd fractions—16ths, 32nds, etc. are required. Also called "Stack Fractions."

Piece Fractions

These are EN and EM versions with only the denominators. The numerators are "created" using special numerals, such as the superiors, which position with the denominator to form the full fraction.

Phony Fractions

Just use the normal numerals separated by a slash when you need a fraction but don't have it. Make sure you use a hyphen to make 1 1/4 look like 1-1/4.

Decimal fractions

¼ = .25 and so on.

And, of course, you can spell the fraction out: ¼ = one quarter.

Piece Fractions

1/12   1/16   15/32   45/64

EN $\frac{1}{4}$ $\frac{1}{2}$ $\frac{3}{4}$ $\frac{1}{8}$ $\frac{3}{8}$ $\frac{5}{8}$ $\frac{7}{8}$ $\frac{1}{3}$

EM

¼   ½   ¾   ⅛   ⅜

Phony   1/4

g

Galley

Greek

Gutter

Galley

Refers to a length of typeset material; a take. In hot metal, a metal tray with raised edges held about 20" of metal type. This much material was then proofed and handled so as to divide jobs into workable units.

The term came to refer both to the amount of material and its state. Since a galley proof was made right after type was set, it was a "first" or "reading" proof. Subsequently, the material would be corrected and organized into pages, creating "final" or "page" or "repro" proofs.

Thus, a galley is a rough proof or copy of a length of typeset material. Today, galleys are not usually of equal lengths.

---

29 JOB 6120 -0009-02 QUOTES/8
REV:09-21 EXP:09-16 AD SIZ: 299.10

■

Quotes

Quotes are opening and closing punctuation marks to indicate verbal statements or to define or emphasize certain words. Double quotes are normally used, with single quotes used within a double quote quote, as in "Doubles on the outside, 'singles' on the inside." The close quote is an apostrophe.

Quotation marks (or quotes) were originally commas only, usually placed in the outer margin, applied by Morel of Paris in 1557. A century later they looked like the present so-called French Quotes (<< >>) which were placed in the center of the type body so that the same character could be used for either the open or closed position. English printers refused to use the French form and inverted the comma at the beginning and used the apostrophes at the close. Of course, they were not symmetrical. It has long been recommended that a hair space (less than a Thin Space—perhaps the equivalent of today's Unit space) is used to separate the quotes from certain letters:

'These are too close . . .
"These look better . . .
"And these don't need them . . .

"But 'Be warned to use them between multiple quotes.'"

Usually the punctuation at the end negates the need for additional space at the close.

Greek

Used mainly in math, but often appears in other instances. Remember, there is an upper and lower case.

Upper case	Lower case	Description
A	α	alpha
B	β	beta **(bay-ta)**
X	χ	chi
Δ	δ	delta
E	ε	epsilon
H	η	eta **(ate-a)**
Γ	γ	gamma
I	ι	iota
K	κ	kappa
Λ	λ	lambda
M	μ	mu **(moo)**
N	ν	nu **(noo)**
Ω	ω	omega
O	o	omicron
Φ	φ	phi **(fee)**
Π	π	pi
Ψ	ψ	psi **(p-sea)**
P	ρ	rho
Σ	σ ς	sigma
T	τ	tau
Θ	θ	theta **(thay-ta)**
Υ	υ	upsilon
Ξ	ξ	xi **(Ksee)**
Z	ζ	zeta **(zay-ta)**

Gutter

The space between columns of type. Usually determined by the number and width of columns and the overall width of the area to be filled. Sometimes a rule is used instead of blank space.

Gutters should not be too narrow so that columns run together. In these narrow cases, the rule line is most often used.

h

| *Hairline* |
| *Hyphenation* |
| *Homograph* |

Hairline

Perhaps the thinnest possible line that can be printed. Typeface characters may include hairline elements (stems, serifs, etc.), especially script typefaces.

Care should be used in applying hairlines, and the printing requirement should be considered. Reverses or overprints could present problems.

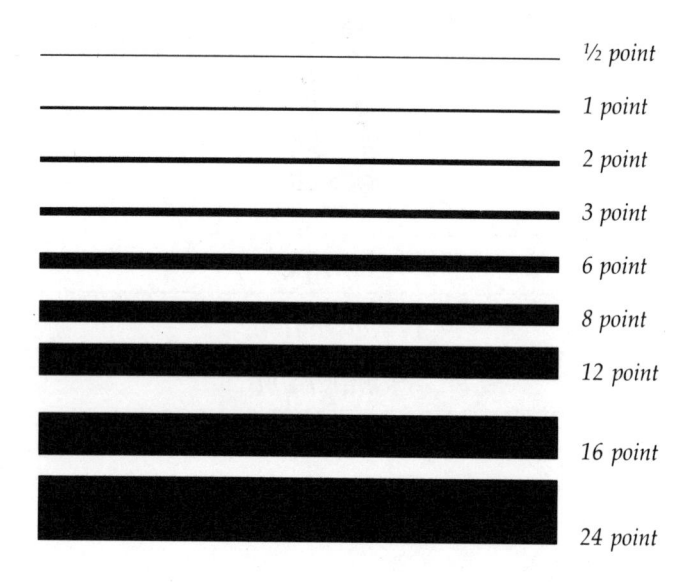

———————————————————— ½ point
———————————————————— 1 point
———————————————————— 2 point
———————————————————— 3 point
———————————————————— 6 point
———————————————————— 8 point
———————————————————— 12 point
———————————————————— 16 point
———————————————————— 24 point

Ths is Avant Garde Light

A hairline typeface

Hyphenation

Breaking a word into syllables and inserting hyphens, manually or automatically, so that word spaces remain consistent, within prescribed limits, for proper justification.

The basic rules for hyphenation are:
1. There must be at least two characters on either side of the hyphen point.
2. Numerals should not be hyphenated (but they could be in an "emergency" at a comma point).
3. It is not good practice to hyphenate in a headline.
4. Never hyphenate a one syllable word.
5. Divide on a double consonant, unless the word root ends with a double consonant (e.g. "miss-ing").
6. Not more than three hyphens in a row.

An incorrect word division is called a "bad break."

Here is a typical set of commands for establishing the hyphenation requirement:

AH0—Allows no hyphenation at all.

AH1—Allows hyphenation of all words except compound words such as *mother-in-law*.

AH2—Allows hyphenation of all words, with compound words breaking only at hyphen.

AH3—Allows full hyphenation capability of all words, including compound words.

AH4—Allows no hyphenation at all except at text hyphens, slashes and em dashes.

An associated command might override the "maximum hyphens in a row" in order to preserve letter/word space consistency.

A *discretionary hyphen* (DH) is inserted in a word during input to give the system a specific point to hyphenate, and that point will take precedence over any logic-generated point. Often, the DH at the beginning of a word tells the system not to hyphenate the word at all.

Text set allowing 2 hyphens in a row

The National Safety Council has announced a new program of financial grants and recognition to non-governmental organizations and individuals who are conducting programs to curb the drinking driver menace. The grants to organizations, individuals, and institutions are funded by General Motors Foundation, Inc., and the Mobil Foundation, Inc. The Council is setting up a panel to consider entries for the grant program, with the following criteria: action must be directly related to the drinking driver problem;

Text set with no hyphenation

The National Safety Council has announced a new program of financial grants and recognition to non-governmental organizations and individuals who are conducting programs to curb the drinking driver menace. The grants to organizations, individuals, and institutions are funded by General Motors Foundation, Inc., and the Mobil Foundation, Inc. The Council is setting up a panel to consider entries for the grant program, with the following criteria: action must be directly related to the drinking driver problem;

Homographs

Homographs are those annoying words that are spelled the same, but pronounced and hyphenated differently. (Homonyms are those words that are only pronounced the same, e.g. red and read.) The process of hyphenation in America is based upon pronunciation (in England they based it upon the word's derivation). Computer programs that hyphenate automatically cannot effectively handle homographs because the computer would have to derive the meaning of the words. In any case, the hyphenation of these words depends upon the mind of the person whose fingers are dancing o'er the keyboard. Here is our list. The italic version is the most common form.

ac-er-ous	ace-rous	*hal-ter*	halt-er
ad-ept	adept	*hind-er*	hin-der
agape	aga-pe	*ho-mer*	hom-er
an-chor-ite	an-cho-rite	*hurt-er*	hur-ter
ar-sen-ic	ar-se-nic	*im-pugn-a-ble*	im-pug-na-ble
as-so-ciate	as-so-ci-ate	*in-val-id*	in-va-lid
bun-ter	bunt-er	*lea-guer*	leagu-er
bus-ses	buss-es	*le-gate*	leg-ate
butter	butt-er	*lim-ber*	limb-er
chaf-er	cha-fer	*lus-ter*	lust-er
chaf-fer	chaff-er	*mas-ter*	mast-er
chart-er	char-ter	*min-ute*	mi-nute
cor-ner	corn-er	*nes-tling*	nest-ling
cor-se-let	corse-let	*pe-tit*	pet-it
cos-ter	cost-er	*pe-ri-odic*	per-iod-ic
cra-ter	crat-er	*pin-ky*	pink-y
deca-meter	de-cam-e-ter	*pla-ner*	plan-er
de-nier	de-ni-er	*pray-er*	prayer
de-sert	des-ert	*pre-ce-dent*	prec-e-dent
di-vers	div-ers	*pre-sent (v.)*	pres-ent (n.)
dos-ser	doss-er	*pro-ject (v.)*	proj-ect (n.)
drap-er	dra-per	*prod-uce (n.)*	pro-duce (v.)
el-lip-ses	el-lips-es	*prod-uct*	pro-duct
er-go-tism	er-got-ism	*prog-ress (n.)*	pro-gress (v.)
eve-ning	even-ing	*putt-er*	put-ter
for-mer	form-er	*put-ting*	putt-ing
foun-der	found-er	*raf-ter*	raft-er
full-er	ful-ler	*reb-el*	re-bel
gaf-fer	gaff-er	*re-cord*	rec-ord
gain-er	gai-ner	*ref-use*	re-fuse
gai-ter	gait-er	*re-sume*	re-su-me
ge-net	gen-et	*ro-sier*	ros-ier
ge-ni-al	ge-nial	*spill-er*	spil-ler
glid-er	gli-der	*sta-ter*	stat-er
grain-ing	grai-ning	*stin-gy*	stingy
grop-er	gro-per	*stov-er*	sto-ver
grou-per	group-er	*tamp-er*	tam-per
grous-er	grou-ser	*ten-ter*	tent-er
		wel-ter	welt-er

i

Ideograph
Indention
Inline
Initial
Italic

Ideograph

The ideograph or ideogram is a symbol that represents an idea. The skull and crossbones represents death. A Chinese or Japanese ideograph can represent things as ideas or both.

Indention

Not called "indentation." A form of placement for text and display showing the relation of items, one to another.

The simplest indent is the *paragraph*, which denotes the beginning of a text block. The indent should be proportional to the line length:

Under 24 picas—1 EM space

25–36 picas—1½ EM spaces

37 picas or more—2 EM spaces

It should be noted that the EM space is the width of the point size, and if heads of a different size from the text are used the EM will not allow the same width indent. One should change to the most common point size before calling for the EM.

Head

*This is a text line. Use a
10 point EM at the start of "Head" line.*

A *hanging* indent is the reverse of a paragraph indent, with the first line to the full measure and subsequent lines in the paragraph indented.

Both of these indents apply primarily to blocks of copy and may be indented from the left, right or both margins.

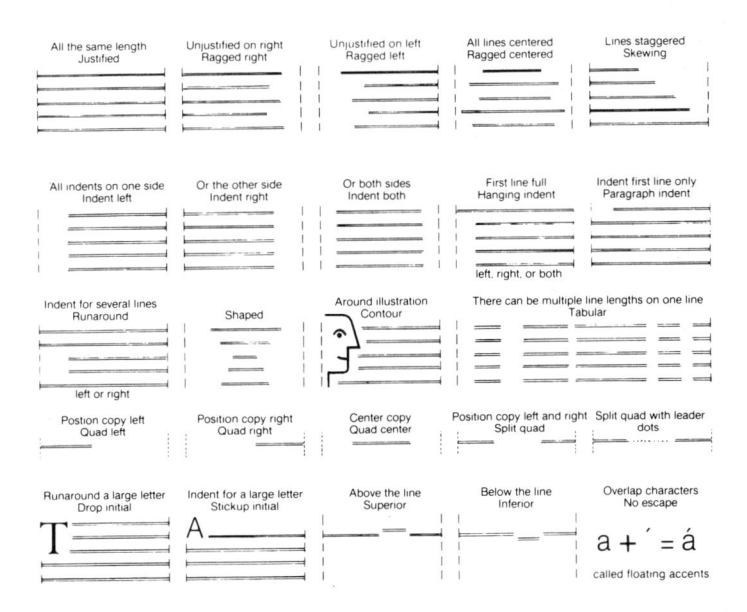

All the same length Justified	Unjustified on right Ragged right	Unjustified on left Ragged left	All lines centered Ragged centered	Lines staggered Skewing
All indents on one side Indent left	Or the other side Indent right	Or both sides Indent both	First line full Hanging indent	Indent first line only Paragraph indent

left, right, or both

Indent for several lines Runaround	Shaped	Around illustration Contour	There can be multiple line lengths on one line Tabular

left or right

Postion copy left Quad left	Position copy right Quad right	Center copy Quad center	Position copy left and right Split quad	Split quad with leader dots

Runaround a large letter Drop initial	Indent for a large letter Stickup initial	Above the line Superior	Below the line Inferior	Overlap characters No escape
T	A			a + ´ = á

called floating accents

73

Inline

A type style that resembles a chisel effect as if chipped out of stone.

These are classic in their appearance and should be used in small doses for major display purposes. They are especially well suited to drop out from a dark background.

ABCDEFGHIJKLMNOPQRSTUVW
XYZ (&.,:;!?"",-°$¢%/£) 1234567890

Caslon Inline

ABCDEFGHIJ
KLMNOPQRS
TUVWXYZ
&(.,:;)?!:abcdefff
fiflffifflghijklm
nopqrstuvwxyz
$1234567890¢
c/$% 01234567890

Bodoni Open

AABCDEFFG
HIJKLLMNO
PPQRSTTUV
VWWXYYZ
&(.,:;"" !?)*abcd
efghijklmnop
qrstuvwxyz
$1234567
890£¢/%$

1234567890(wv)

Antique Roman

Initial

Initial letters are sometimes used at the beginning of chapters or paragraphs. The first style, and historically the oldest, is the sunken or "drop cap" position. Here the initial letter is set down within the copy, not rising above the top line of the text. The second style is the raised or "stick up" initial, and it rests on the base-line of the first or subsequent line of text and rises above the top line of the text.

The most important aspect in the use of initial letters is *fit*. Here are the major considerations:

1. Square or contoured format
2. Left margin should be aligned or indented
3. Left margin aligned or optically aligned
4. Cap lead-in or small cap lead-in or lowercase lead-in
5. Related or non-related type style

MANY of these initials look terrible for one major reason. The space on the right of the initial must optically match the leading space at the bottom. The initial must base align and the first word should be cap or small cap and moved over slightly to show relationship.

Note that the space around the initial letter should be the same on the side as it is on the bottom.

A square letter like this is easily handled, but DECORATIVE initials, used with machine matter, are first measured to allow for the initial, the lines are then cast with the necessary blank spaces, the slugs are next sawed to measure, and then the initial finally is justified into position alongside the opening lines of the first paragraph.

Some letters require "contouring."

ALINE beginning with the article *A* or the pronoun *I* requires the normal wordspacing between the initial and the first word of the line. Correct spacing at the side of the A is shown in connection with this paragraph. Good printing practice requires that the initial be followed at the bottom by at least two full lines of type.

LETTERS like *L* and *A* require special treatment in order to tie in properly with the remaining letters of the first word of the paragraph. Certain letters will require considerable mortising to obtain close contact of type and initial.

Here the initial letter extends slightly into the left margin to optically line-up.

FOR "fine" printing something is required in addition to care—certain vital gifts of the mind and understanding. Only when these are added to a knowledge of the technical processes will there result a piece of design, i. e. a work expressing logic, consistency, and personality. Fine printing may be described as the product of a lively and seasoned intelligence working with carefully chosen type, ink, and paper. First it must be borne in mind that

In all cases the letter must align at the base of a line of text.

THE USE of an ornamental scroll before the opening initial is a novel way of adding to the attractiveness of composition deserving of this extra consideration.

OCCASIONALLY, a simple ornamental stroke, such as here used, will do much to lift the composition out of the commonplace.

With a raised initial letter, it must also rest on the baseline and kerning should be applied where necessary.

The use of an initial followed by lower case is occasionally seen, but such a practice is hardly one to be recommended to the beginner.

Raised letters may also be indented.

Illustrating the correct method of handling raised initials. With machine matter, the raised initial is cut in and aligned with the lower edge of the type face of the first word of the paragraph.

If quotes are to be set, they should be in a size between the text size and the initial letter size. They may even be eliminated.

When I was an apprentice," he said, "a foreman would frequently insist that opening quotes were unnecessary with initials."

Opening quotes omitted.

"Today," he continued, "it would be difficult to find a good printer condoning such slipshod methods of composition."

Opening quotes in margin.

The initial cap may rest on the baseline and rise above the text (as illustrated above) and this is done with a simple point size change, or mixed in with the text so that the copy is indented around the initial cap (see above). Traditionally, the first word following the initial should be in small caps or capitals.

Also note that the type should contour the initial cap. Since this is difficult to do in some cases, a simple indent is set up and the character positioned by use of the No Flash/No Escape functions.

The Initials of the DeVinne Press

SINGLE LETTERS

Italic

Refers to the slant of characters in a particular typeface, to the right. This is a variation in posture.

In 1500 the *italic* as a typeface was developed. Aldus Manutius adapted the cursive handwriting used in the Papal Chancery and paid Griffo to cut punches in that style. At first the style was called "corsiva" (cursive) or "cancellarsca" (chancery). Sometimes it is called the "Italian hand." In Germany, "Kursiv" is used instead of "italic." Like the word "roman," the word "italic" credits Italy as the land of origin. It was coined by the French and was not capitalized.

Aldus did not intend italic for emphasis, its primary use today. He had it cut because it was narrower than the roman, and he could get more words on a page to produce a book he could sell cheaper. Later, roman styles were designed narrower, and italic, as a text style, was too hard to read, never became a standard typeface.

Robert Granjon, who worked for Garamond, cut about ten styles for Christopher Plantin of Antwerp (1520–89). One of these became the model for an italic style designed as a *companion* to a roman style (called a *sympathetic* italic). It was a different alphabet, closer to handwriting than the roman, and appearing to link letters.

There are three kinds of italics. *Unrelated* italics are "pure" styles based on Fifteenth-century "hands." *Related* italics are designed to blend with a specific roman typeface, but still more or less "pure" italic. *Matching* italics are essentially the same design as a particular roman typeface. Digitized typesetting devices that modify characters electronically to create the italic are creating matching italics, although purists will call them "oblique."

While the slant of the italic will vary, a good standard is about 78°. Today it is used for emphasis, titles, quotes and extracts. Certain characters may change form when they make the transition from roman to italic.

Tilting characters to the left (back slant) or right (oblique) so as to change their posture is called slant. This is optical or electronic distortion and is different from a true italic.

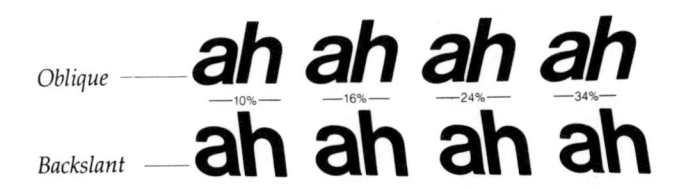

Oblique — *ah* *ah* *ah* *ah*
—10%— —16%— —24%— —34%—

Backslant — ah ah ah ah

As far as typography is concerned, the terms "italic," "cursive," and "oblique" all mean the same thing: the slanted version of a given typeface. Italic is still the preferred term in English-speaking countries and in France. Most other countries, however, use the term "cursive," which means running or flowing.

The term "oblique" was most commonly associated with the Futura or sans serif family of typefaces. In this case, oblique is used rather than italic or cursive because the designer, Paul Renner, felt that the Futura italic was not a "true" italic and that is should have a name that more accurately described it. So he called it "oblique," which simply means slanted.

Modern digitized typesetters can electronically slant characters to create "oblique" fonts. Oblique refers to a more slanting of characters; however, italic faces are designed along more calligraphic lines.

In markup, italic is indicated by an underline.

Copy to be put in italic:
1. Titles of publications.
2. names of ships, trains, aircraft.
3. Foreign words and phrases.
4. Scientific names.
5. Mathematical unknowns.
6. Protagonists in legal citations.
7. Words quoted by name.
8. Quotations.
9. Names of shows or plays (but not TV shows—use quotes).
10. Works of art.

Alternatives for italic for highlighting or emphasizing are the quotes or an underline.

All capital italic lines are to be avoided.

j
Justification

Justification

Typing or setting text lines to the same length so that they line up on the left *and* the right. The practice originated with Mediaeval scribes who ruled margins and text lines so as to speed writing and fit as many characters on a line as possible.

Later, metal type required *even* copy blocks to allow "lock up" into page form. The opposite of justified text is ragged text.

Justifcation is accomplished by filling a line until the last possible word or syllable fits and then dividing the remaining space by the number of word spaces. The result is placed at each word space.

Word spaces are variable in width, expanding or contracting as needed to space the line out to its justification width.

Margins are the imaginary vertical demarcations for text or tabular columns. Overall or primary margins are established by the line length function or the cumulative total of secondary margins (tab or text columns).

Justified

MARGIN   MARGIN

This section demonstrates justified copy. Note that each line has been set to the same width, hyphenated where necessary and that the spaces between words vary. Justified copy must end with some *quadding* or *end-of-paragraph* command.

Ragged Right

MARGIN   MARGIN

This section demonstrates ragged right copy. Note that hyphenation is rarely used and that all word spaces are the same width. The command used to accopmlish this was [rr. A *quad left* command must end ragged right lines.

Ragged Center

MARGIN   MARGIN

This section demonstrates ragged center copy. Note that each line is automatically centered and that all word spaces are the same width. The command used to accomplish this was [rc. A ragged center take must end with a *quad center* command.

Ragged Left

MARGIN   MARGIN

This section demonstrates ragged left copy. Note that all word spaces are the same width. The command used to accomplish this was [rl. A *quad right* command must be used to end a ragged left take.

k

Kerning

Kerning

The use of negative letterspacing between certain character combinations in order to reduce the space between them is Kerning. Characters in typesetting have specific width values and are actually positioned within an imaginary rectangle:

Below, right side wall of the W will touch the left side wall of the a, but because of the shape of these two letters, a space will result:

Wa Wa Wa Wa Wa
Ha Ha Ha Ha Ha

In kerning, the space is reduced by "fooling" the typesetting machine. We subtract a certain number of units from the width of the W and the typesetter positioning system then moves less units than would normally be required and the subsequent letter "overlaps" to visually reduce the intercharacter space.

Topographic Kerning is a new concept which defines characters in terms of their *shape* as well as their width. Thus a compute could *match* shapes on an almost infinite basis.

Most present computer typesetting systems can kern over 200 character pairs automatically. We are concerned about this because of one major factor. After you have taken care of the 20 or so primary pairs, you then are limited to a few hundered, and, if you do those hundred you should do several hundred more, and thus you will be creating a situation of inconsistency. If you cannot kern *infinitely*, then you may as well stay with the top 20—anything after that is a numbers game.

AC AT AV AW AY FA LT LV LW LY OA OV OW OY PA TA TO VA VO WA WO YA YO Av Aw Ay A' A- A— F. F, F- F-
L' L- L— P. P, P; P: P- P— R- R— Ta Te Ti To Tr Tu Tw Ty T. T, T; T: T- T— Va Ve Vi Vo Vu V. V, V; V: V- V— Wa We Wi
Wo Wr Wu Wy W. W, W; W: W- W— Ya Ye Yi Yo Yu Y. Y, Y; Y: Y- Y— ff fi fl rm rn rt ry r. r, r- r— y. y, .' .' 'S 's " "
AG AO AQ AU BA BE BL BP BR BU BV BW BY CA CO CR DA DD DE DI DL DM DN DO DP DR DU DV DW DY
EC EO FC FG FO GE GO GR GU HO IC IG IO JA JO KO LC LG LO LU MC MG MO NC NG NO OB OD OE OF
OH OI OK OL OM ON OP OR OT OU OX PE PL PO PP PU PY QU RC RG RO RT RU RV RW RY SI SM ST SU TC
UA UC UG UO US VC VG VS WC WG YC YS ZO Ac Ad Ae Ag Ao Ap Aq At Au Bb Bi Bk Bl Br Bu By B. B, Ca Cr
C. C, Da D. D, Eu Ev Fa Fe Fi Fo Fr Ft Fu Fy F; F: Gu He Ho Hu Hy Ic Id Iq Io It Ja Je Jo Ju J. J, Ke Ko Ku K- K— Lu
Ly Ma Mc Md Me Mo Mu Na Ne Ni No Nu N. N, Oa Ob Oh Ok Ol O. O, Pa Pe Po Rd Re Ro Rt Ru Si Sp Su S. S,
Ua Ug Um Un Up Us U. U, Wd Wm Wt Yd ac ad ae ag ap af at au av aw ay ap bl br bu by b. b, ca ch ck da dc de
dg do dt du dv dw dy d. d, ea ei el em en ep er et eu ev ew ey e. e, fa fe fo f. f, ga ge gh gl go gg g. g, hc hd he hg
ho hp ht hu hv hw hy ic id ie ig io ip it iu iv ja je jo ju j. j, ka kc kd ke kg ko la lc ld le lg lo lp lq lf lu lv lw ly ma
mc md me mg mo mp mt mu mv my nc nd ne ng no np nt nu nv nw ny ob of oh oj ok ol om on op or ou ov ow ox oy
o. o, pa ph pi pl pp pu p. p, qu q. ra rd re rg rk rl ro rq rr rv sh st su s. s, td ta te to t. t, ua uc ud ue ug uo up uq ut
uv uw uy va vb vc vd ve vg vo vv vy v. v, v- v— wa wc wd we wg wh wo w. w, w- w— xe ya yc yd ye yo y- y— 'A '. ',

500 + kern pairs

In hot metal, the kerned combinations had to be combined on one matrix. Here is the set that resulted:

FA PA TA VA WA YA Th Wh

F. P. Ta To Tr Tu Tw Ty T. Va Ve Vo V. Wa
We Wi Wo Wr W. Ya Ye Yo Y.

*F. P. Ta To Tr Tu Tw Ty T. Va Ve Vo V. Wa
We Wi Wo Wr W. Ya Ye Yo Y.*

fa fe fo fr fs ft fu fy ffa ffe ffo ffr ffs ffu ffy f,
f. f- ff, ff. ff-

*fa fe fo fr fs ft fu fy ffa ffe ffo ffr ffs ffu ffy f,
f. f- ff, ff. ff- f ff*

Kerning is an "optical function." The space between certain letter combinations is reduced until it *looks right*.

Top Twenty Kerns

1. Yo
2. We
3. To
4. Tr
5. Ta
6. Wo
7. Tu
8. Tw
9. Ya
10. Te
11. P.
12. Ty
13. Wa
14. yo
15. we
16. T.
17. Y.
18. TA
19. PA
20. WA

HE — *Requires the least or no kerning*

GL — *Requires minimal kerning*

OC — *Requires moderate kerning*

TA — *Requires maximum kerning*

l

Leaders
Legibility
Letterspacing
Ligature
Line Length
Line Spacing
Logo
Lowercase

Leaders

Essentially dots or dashes which "lead" the eye from one side of a line to the other. In hot metal, leaders were unique characters, with one leader dot centered on an EN width or two leader dots set on an EM width. The dots come in varying weights, ranging from fine, light dots to heavy, bold dots.

The Lincaster provided various styles of leaders to meet differing publishing and printing conditions. They varied primarily in weight of dot or stroke, in dots or strokes to the em, and in hot metal, in depth of punching:

Regular Leaders varied in weight of dot or stroke to match the face and point size with which they are to be used. They are supplied in dot or hyphen style in two, four or six dots or strokes to the em.

Universal Leaders had a uniform weight of dot or stroke in 4- to 14-point sizes, regardless of the typeface with which they were to be used.

Primarily intended for book and jobbing work, they were supplied in dot or hyphen style—the dot in two, four or six dots to the em, the hyphen in two or four strokes to the em.

Thin Leaders were used with either the Regular or Universal style (four dots or strokes to em) for close justification, when one spaceband is used in the line. Supplied in quarter-em widths in 8- to 14-point sizes.

Newspaper Leaders were the "regular" dot or hyphen leader and are supplied in two dots or strokes to the em. They vary in weight to match the face and point size with which they are to be used.

Radial Leaders were primarily for newspaper use, with a uniform weight of dot in all point sizes, and were made with a rounded or radial printing surface to prevent perforating paper and damaging press blankets.

Oversize Leaders had uniform weight of dot (.018) in 4- to 8-point sizes and uniform weight of dot (.21) in 9- to 14-point sizes regardless of type face with which they are to be used. Supplied one dot to en and two dots to em.

Dash Leaders were en- and em-width hairline dashes (.004 in weight) punched to cast type high and present a continuous, unbroken line. Essential for tabular work, where dash of figure width is necessary.

Leader Aligning Dashes cast a continuous, unbroken line for jobbing work. Punched to cast type high and supplied in four widths: 2, 3, 6 and 12 points, in all standard alignments. Available in four weights of line: hairline .004, half-point .007, one-point .014, or two-point .028.

Today, the period is used most often as the leader dot. Unfortunately, it does not always work well. For instance, one might find better looking leaders by going to a lower point size, instead of setting the leader dots in the same size as the text.

Leaders must align vertically as well as horizontally and this is usually done automatically by the machine. One of the problems faced with leaders is related to the mathematics of dividing their width into the line length. A 9-point leader, for instance, would divide into a 20 pica line (20 × 12 = 240 points divided by 9 =) 26.66 times. The blank space that results must be placed somewhere and machines may not put it where it looks best.

Therefore:

1. Select the narrowest possible width that will achieve the look desired. The en is most popular.

2. Key a word space at the beginning or end of the line, as a place for the excess space to go.

3. Reduce to a smaller point size.

This will result in allowing more leaders to fit on a line and provide for remainder space.

Legibility

A poet once said that legibility was the "certainty of deciphering." It certainly has to do with ease of reading, and perception of the message communicated.

Legibility has been reflected in the design of letterforms to aid in the above. Large x-height, serif faces with a bolder print to them tend to score highly in legibility research results. Additionally, we have learned that word spacing should be the width of a lowercase "i" and the leading should be slightly larger than the word spacing.

You can control legibility by proper typographic practice.

Legibility is based upon the way we read. The human eye makes a fixation each quarter of a second and "takes in" a group of words. It then jumps to the next fixation, etc. Each of these fixations is called a *saccad* and *saccadic jumps move the eye from saccad point to saccad point*. Speed reading approaches usually try to train you to make larger "jumps" and take in more words at one time.

Thus, legibility research teaches us that narrower line lengths, consistent word spacing and well-designed typefaces will aid in more efficient reading—readability.

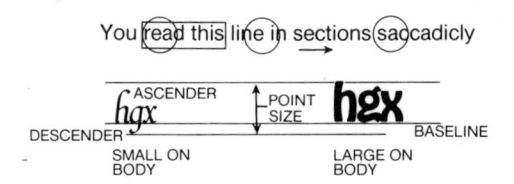

You read this line in sections saccadicly

ASCENDER
hgx — POINT SIZE — hgx
DESCENDER — BASELINE
SMALL ON BODY — LARGE ON BODY

The upper portion of a line of type is easier to read than the lower portion.

The upper portion of a line of type is easier to read than the lower portion.

Our eyes travel along the X-height.

The lower portion of a line of type is more difficult to read than the upper portion.

The lower portion of a line of type is more difficult to read than the upper portion.

Letterspacing

Very simply the space between letters. It comes in two varieties—positive and negative.

Positive Letterspacing

Here, space is *added* between letters in the same increment for one or more of the following reasons:

1. Automatic letterspacing activated so that word spaces are not too wide during justification. Called into action when word spaces reach a pre-set maximum amount.

2. Selective letterspacing for character combinations (such as rn, which might look like an m) that might be too tight.

3. Word or line letterspacing for aesthetic reasons, such as all capital titles or headings.

Negative Letterspacing

Space is *subtracted* from between letters in the same increment:

1. Tight spacing (or white space reduction) is required for artistic reasons.

2. Selective subtraction (kerning) for certain character combinations.

Kern can be a noun or a verb . . . or even an adjective. It reduces space between characters and can cause some of them to overlap.

Touching
Typography Typography

Very tight
Typography Typography

Tight
Typography Typography

Normal
Typography Typography

tv
Typography Typography

Foundry
Typography Typography

LETTERS ARE SPACED	**6** (T1) Expertype blends advanced technology with quality typography to attain t (T2) Expertype blends advanced technology with quality typography to attain the p (T3) Expertype blends advanced technology with quality typography to attain the pe
LETTERS ARE SPACED	
LETTERS ARE SPACED	**7** (T1) Expertype blends advanced technology with quality typography (T2) Expertype blends advanced technology with quality typography to (T3) Expertype blends advanced technology with quality typography to at
LETTERS ARE SPACED	**8** (T1) Expertype blends advanced technology with quality typ (T2) Expertype blends advanced technology with quality typog (T3) Expertype blends advanced technology with quality typogra
LETTERS ARE SPACED	
LETTERS ARE SPACED	**9** (T1) Expertype blends advanced technology with qua (T2) Expertype blends advanced technology with qualit (T3) Expertype blends advanced technology with quality t
LETTERS ARE SPACED	
LETTERS ARE SPACED	**10** (T1) Expertype blends advanced technology with (T2) Expertype blends advanced technology with q (T3) Expertype blends advanced technology with qu
LETTERS ARE SPACED	
LETTERS ARE SPACED	**11** (T1) Expertype blends advanced technology (T2) Expertype blends advanced technology w (T3) Expertype blends advanced technology witl
LETTERS ARE SPACED	
LETTERS ARE SPACED	**12** (T1) Expertype blends advanced technolog (T2) Expertype blends advanced technology (T3) Expertype blends advanced technology v
LETTERS ARE SPACED	
LETTERS ARE SPACED	**14** (T1) Expertype blends advanced tech (T2) Expertype blends advanced techn (T3) Expertype blends advanced techno
LETTERS ARE SPACED	**16** (T1) Expertype blends advanced (T2) Expertype blends advanced te (T3) Expertype blends advanced tec
LETTERS ARE SPACED	
LETTERS ARE SPACED	**18** (T1) Expertype blends advanc (T2) Expertype blends advance (T3) Expertype blends advanced
LETTERS ARE SPACED	
LETTERS ARE SPACED	**20** (T1) Expertype blends adva (T2) Expertype blends advar (T3) Expertype blends advanc
LETTERS ARE SPACED	
LETTERS ARE SPACED	**24** (T1) Expertype blends a (T2) Expertype blends ac (T3) Expertype blends ad
LETTERS ARE SPACED	

The concept of tracking is simply "organized negative letterspacing." The typesetter or supplier has determined three or more levels of negative letterspacing to allow you to select the right "look" or "color."

Ligature

Two or more characters designed as a distinct unit. Should be used in headlines sparingly. There are five f-ligatures plus the diphthongs. Gutenberg's font had many "ligatures" in order to simulate handwriting.

fi ff fl ffi ffl

The traditional ligatures are easily and automatically generated on command. Although book production most often finds them mandatory, advertising typography rarely finds them useful—and, in fact, they cannot be used in copy set tighter than normal spacing.

This automation will allow *any* ligature to be selected without operator intervention—an incentive for the expansion of ligature design and use . . . until we someday return to a modern version of the Gutenberg font.

The diphthongs ae and oe, æ and œ, are also considered ligatures.

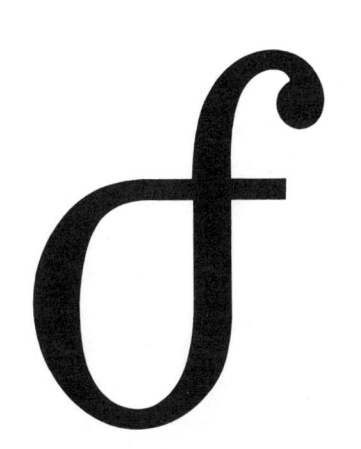

Gutenberg's font had many ligatures to emulate handwriting.

Someone once created a more contemporary set of ligatures.

93

Line Length

The area between two margins. Text copy should adhere to certain time-tested rules for length of line in order to achieve maximum readability.

Type Size	Minimum Length	Optimum Length	Maximum Length
6	8	10	12
7	8	11	14
8	9	13	16
9	10	14	18
10	13	16	20
11	13	18	22
12	14	21	24
14	18	24	28
16	21	27	32
18	24	30	36

Sometimes the formula *Font size* × 2 is used to determine the maximum line length. *Lowercase alphabet* × 1.5 is also used.

Wider faces look best with wider line lengths; condensed faces look best with narrow line lengths. Instead of wide line lengths, double or multiple columns of smaller line lengths should be used.

A line should have 55 to 60 characters or 9 to 10 words for optimum readability. Also, as a line length increases, paragraph indentions should increase, too.

Multiple, narrow columns are preferable to single, wide columns.

Line Spacing

The space between lines of type, called "leading" (pronounced "ledding") or "vertical spacing" or "film advance" should adhere to certain time-tested rules for readability.

Type Size	Minimum Leading	Optimum Leading	Maximum Leading
6	Solid (no lead)	1 point	1 point
7	Solid (no lead)	1 point	1½ points
8	Solid (no lead)	1½ points	2 points
9	Solid	2 points	3 points
10	Solid	2 points	3 points
11	1 point	2 points	3 points
12	2 points	3 points	4 points
14	3 points	4 points	6 points
16	4 points	4 points	6 points
18	5 points	4 points	6 points

Leading should be in proportion to line length and point size—about 20% of the point size, or some say it should be slightly larger than the optimum word space. Very fine spacing was called "carding" in hot metal.

One of the capabilities that modern typesetting techniques makes available is called "minus leading." This means that the type is set with a leading value *less* than the point size, 9 on 8½. Usually, this can only be done with faces that are small on body or have short ascenders/descenders, or for all caps as in heads.

Small x-height faces and some sans serifs should have minimal or minus leading.

To calculate the minimum amount of leading required between two type lines, especially when you are changing point sizes—take ⅓ of the present point size and add it to ⅔ of the point size to be used on the next line. If you do not have the proper leading, the lines could overlap one another.

The most important point to remember: all leading is measured from *baseline to baseline*.

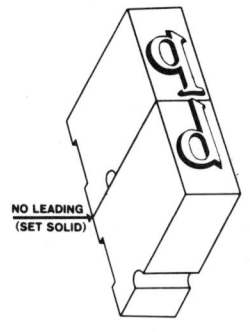

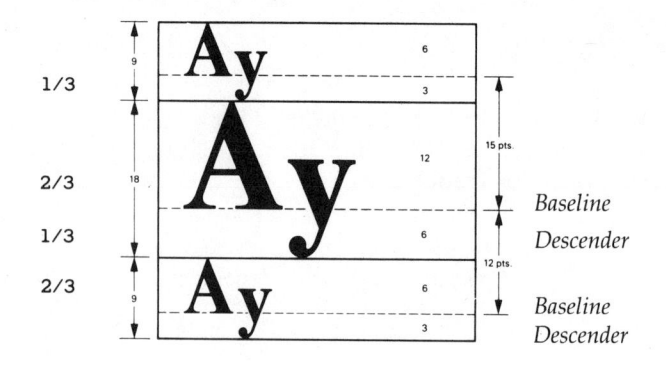

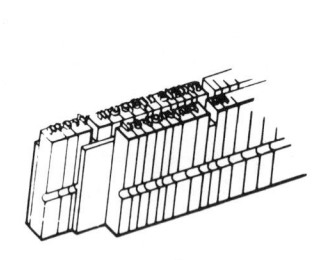

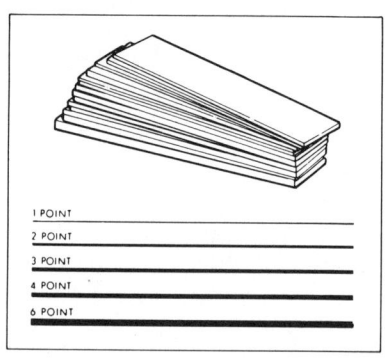

Point Size / Lines Of Type To The Inch (Solid)

Point Size	Lines Of Type To The Inch (Solid)
4	
5	14.4
6	12
7	10.285
8	9
9	8
10	7.2
11	6.545
12	6
14	5.143
16	4.5
18	4
24	3
30	2.4
36	2
42	1.714
48	1.5
72	1

QUICK LEADING CHART

POINT SIZE (FROM)	5	6	7	8	9	10	11	12	14	18	24	30	36	42	48	54	60	72
1/3 POINT SIZE	2	2	3	3	3	3	4	4	5	6	8	10	12	14	16	18	20	24

PLUS

POINT SIZE (FROM)	5	6	7	8	9	10	11	12	14	18	24	30	36	42	48	54	60	72
1/3 POINT SIZE	3	4	4	5	6	7	7	8	9	12	16	20	24	28	32	36	40	48

Quick Formula for Leading

1/3 of point size from + 2/3 of point size to = total leading amount

Logo

A symbol representing a company or product.

Lowercase

The term is derived from the layout of the printer's type case, which had the capital letters in the upper part and the small letters in the lower part.

Lowercase letters evolved as scribes tried to write faster and faster. Two handwriting styles—the *formal* hand of the church and royalty and the *informal* hand of scholars—developed over the centuries. The Caroline minuscule is the direct ancestor of our lowercase.

The evolution of alphabetic characters (or written communication, if you like) was not an organized development. There were three "forces"—Phoenecian, Greek, and Roman—that shaped our alphabet, with the Roman influence being the most important. The beautifully shaped capitals of the Trajan column inspire more of our present generation, than that of Mediaeval Europe. It was more national habits and peculiarities that influenced alphabet characteristics, and only the eventual spread of printing brought "standardization."

Scribes tended two write faster as the demand for written material increased, and thus developed "short cuts" to make serifs and terminal strokes with more *fluid* motions of the pen, instead of separate strokes.

The trend toward *cursive* writing gave both speed (an increase in productivity) and, as a by-product, symmetry, beauty and simplicity. The rapidity of writing brought us the *minuscule*. Up to this point the *uncial* (Latin *uncus*, for crooked) was still a capital letter that rounded the straight lines. The uncial was a *majuscule*. The uncial was, itself, modified in time into the *half uncial* which became the manuscript style of the 8th Century.

Charlemagne inspired the "Caroline" alphabet which a monk named Alcuin designed. It was a true small letter alphabet. The Gothic hand evolved from the Carolingian minuscule. It was the style which Gutenberg used, and the one which the technology of printing spread. The Gothics themselves went through several variations—the Round Gothic, Pointed Gothic, Half Gothic (based on Rotunda). There was also a Cursive Gothic called Schwabacher.

Gothics were also called Textura, since they "wove the texture" of a page, or Blackletter.

None of this was deliberate or organized. Within each geographic area there developed eccentricities. For instance, there were three (or more) Roman hands: the Square Capitals, Rustic Capitals, Everyday Hand, and Roman Cursive. The Uncials evolved from the Rustic and Everyday Hand, where the Half Uncials came more from the Cursive Hand. And is was Charlemagne who decreed that all writing throughout his kingdom—which was in 800 the Holy Roman Empire—were to be recopied in a standard hand: the Caroline Minuscule.

Thus, when printing spread throughout Europe, it became possible to adapt national hands and ressurect many of the characteristics that had been eliminated in the rush for faster handwriting.

In 1585, Louis Elzevir was the first to use "v" and "j" as consonants, and "i" and "u" as vowels. These letters were universally adopted in 1822. Type cases did not have provision for the "j" and "u" and thus they were added after the "z."

Lowercase letters are easier to read because their shapes are distinct, where caps present a monotone appearance in a line.

m

Magnetic Ink Characters
Math

Magnetic Ink Characters

Sometimes called "E13B" characters, they were designed to be deciphered by machines. The ink content allows the machine to "read" the magnetic pattern and then match it to its memory. Note that the characters are designed to eliminate "confusion pairs" so that each pattern will be unique.

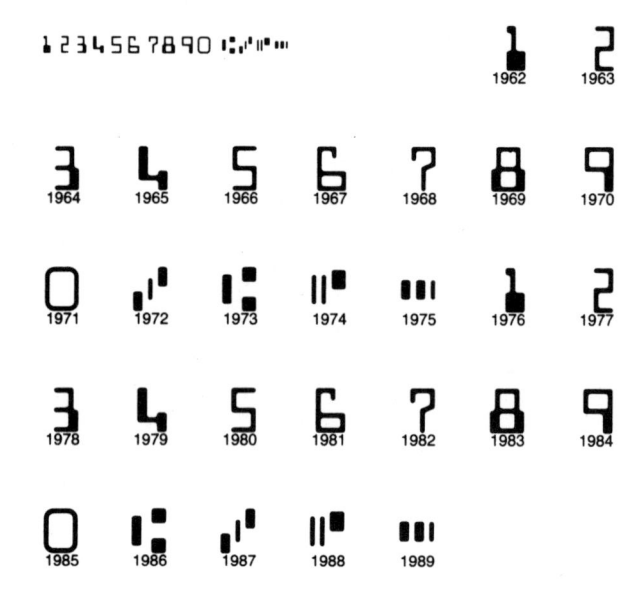

Math

Here are the names for a number of math symbols.

⇌	Geometrically equivalent to
≍	Equivalent to
≃	1) Approximately equal to
	2) Asymptotically equal
	3) Chain homotopic to
≄	Not asymptotically equal
≅	1) Similar to
	2) Geometrically equivalent or congruent to
	3) Equal or nearly equal to
∼	1) Difference between
	2) Is equivalent to
	3) Asymptotic to
	4) Similar to
	5) Of the order of
	6) The complement of
	7) Is not, negation sign (math. logic)
	8) Associate to
≁	1) Is not equivalent to
	2) Is not asymptotic to
	3) Is not similar to
	4) Is not the complement of
≃̇	Is approximately asymptotic to
∽̇	Homothetic (similar and perspective to)
≤	Smaller than
<	Less than
>	Greater than
≮	Not less than
≯	Not greater than
≲	Equivalent to or greater than
≳	Greater than or equivalent to
≵	Not greater than nor equivalent to
≲	Equivalent to or less than
≲	Less than or equivalent to
≳	Greater than, equivalent to or less than
⪅	Less than or approximately equal to
⪆	Greater than or approximately equal to
≪	Much less than
⋘	Much less than
≫	Much greater than
⋙	Much greater than
≪̸	Not much less than
≫̸	Not much greater than
⋘̸	Very much less than
⋙̸	Very much greater than
≶	Less than or greater than (is not equal to)
≷	Greater than or less than (is not equal to)
≦	Less than or equal to
≦	Less than or equal to
≦	Less than or equal to
≰	Not less than nor equal to
#	Congruent and parallel
※	Smash product
◊	1) Between
	2) Quantic, no numerical coefficients
∞	Infinity
⧜	Not infinite
∝	Varies as, proportional to
√	Radical sign
\	End of operation of radical sign (reverse slash)
+	Plus
−	Minus
×	Multiply
÷	Divide
±	Plus or minus
∓	Minus or plus
⊕	Direct sum (group theory)
∔	Direct sum (group theory)
±̊	
⌒	Rotation in negative direction
⌒	Rotation in positive direction
⊞	Plus or equal
⊟	Equal or plus
+₂	Nim-addition
+̂	
⊕	
+̃	Positive difference or sum
+̰	Sum or positive difference
⊞	
⊖	Symmetric difference
⊖	

103

⊗	1) Plethysm operator (group theory)
	2) Convolution product
	3) Direct product
	4) Tensor product
⊗	
⊙	
∞	Most positive
=	1) Equal to
	2) Logical identity
≠	Is not equal to
≢	1) Is not equal to
	2) Logical diversity
≈	1) Approximately equal to
	2) Asymptotic to
	3) Equal to in the mean
	4) Isomorphism
≉	Not asymptotic to
≋	Approximately equal to or equal to
≑	Approximately equal to
≒	Is the image of
≏	Approximately equal to
≅	Approximately equal to or equal to
≧	Greater than or equal to
≥	Greater than or equal to
⩾	Greater than or equal to
≱	Not greater than nor equal to
⋛	Less than, equal to, or greater than
⋝	Greater than, equal to, or less than
≷	Greater than, equal to, or less than
⋚	Less than, greater than, or equal to
⋞	Greater than, less than, or equal to
⋟	Equal to or greater than
⪙	
⪚	
<	
⊲	
⋗	
⋊	
∓	
∗	
≐	1) Approaches the limit
	2) Approaches in value to
≖	
≙	Estimates or is estimated by
≃	

⋏	Is projective with or projective correspondence
⩞	Perspective correspondence
⩜	Equiangular (geometry)
→	1) Approaches or tends to the limit
	2) Implies (math. logic)
	3) Referents of a relation (used thus: $\vec{R}$ math. logic)
	4) Transformation (set theory)
↮	Does not tend to
←	Relata of a relation, used thus $\overleftarrow{R}$
↑	1) Increases monotonically to a limit
	2) Exponent (Algol)
↓	Decreases monotonically to a limit
↕	
⇒	Implies
⇔	1) Implies and is implied by
	2) If and only if
⟹	Convergence
⇐	Is implied by
↔	1) Mutually implies
	2) One-to-one correspondence with
	3) Corresponds reciprocally
	4) Asymptotically equivalent to
	5) If and only if
↮	Does not mutually imply
↠	On to map (Topology)
↣	1 – 1 map
⇆	
⇄	
↻	Clockwise
↺	Anti-clockwise
≻	1) Has a higher rank or order
	2) Contains
⪰	Contains or is equal to
⪯	Is equal to or contains
⊇	Contains or is equal to
≺	Has a lower rank or order
⊀	1) Has not a lower rank or order than
	2) Is not contained in nor equal to
⪯	Is contained in or equal to
⊴	Is contained in or equal to
⋠	Is not contained in nor equal to
≼	Is contained in or is equivalent to
⋘	Has much lower rank or order
▷	Implies
◁	1) Implied by

104

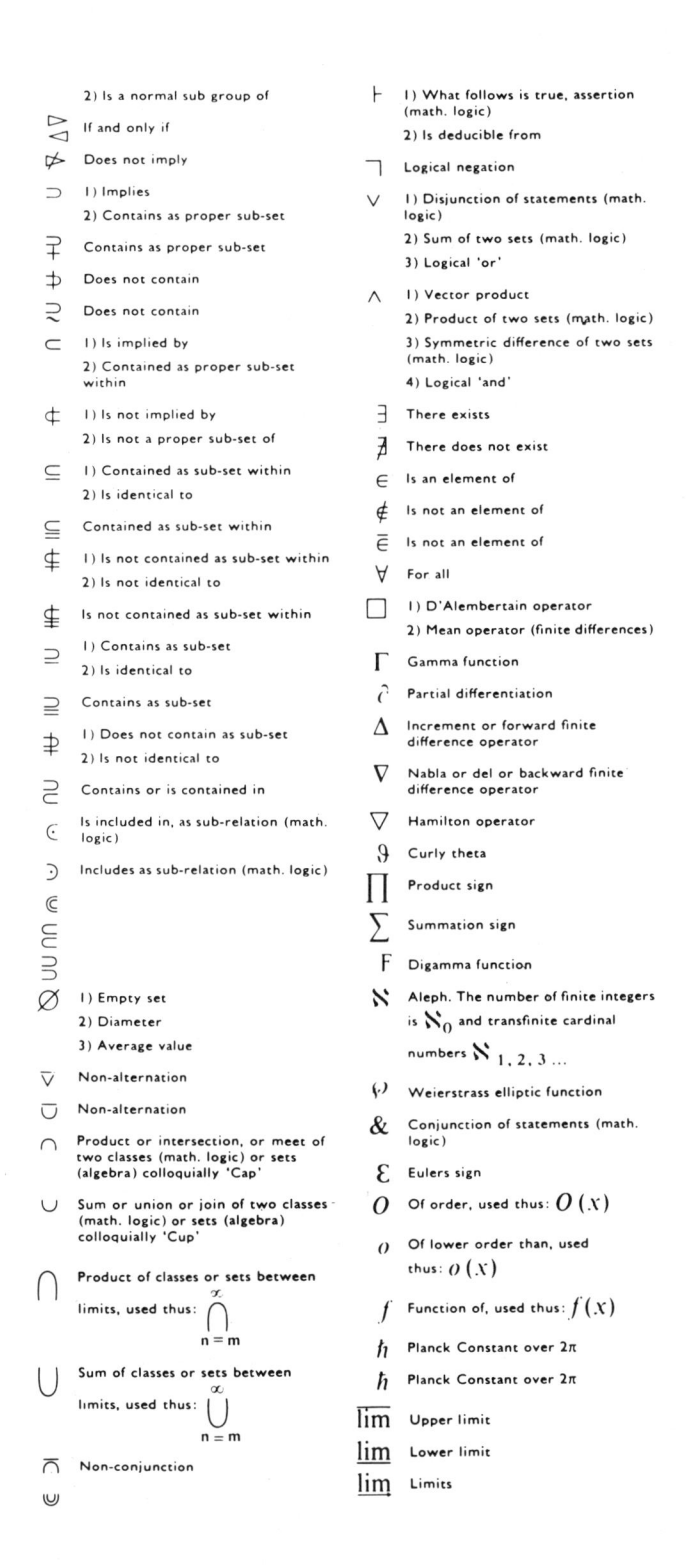

	2) Is a normal sub group of
⊳⊲	If and only if
⊅	Does not imply
⊃	1) Implies
	2) Contains as proper sub-set
⊋	Contains as proper sub-set
⊅	Does not contain
⊉	Does not contain
⊂	1) Is implied by
	2) Contained as proper sub-set within
⊄	1) Is not implied by
	2) Is not a proper sub-set of
⊆	1) Contained as sub-set within
	2) Is identical to
⊆	Contained as sub-set within
⊈	1) Is not contained as sub-set within
	2) Is not identical to
⊈	Is not contained as sub-set within
⊇	1) Contains as sub-set
	2) Is identical to
⊇	Contains as sub-set
⊉	1) Does not contain as sub-set
	2) Is not identical to
⊋	Contains or is contained in
⊂	Is included in, as sub-relation (math. logic)
⊃	Includes as sub-relation (math. logic)
∈	
∋	
⋳	
⋺	
∅	1) Empty set
	2) Diameter
	3) Average value
▽	Non-alternation
⨃	Non-alternation
∩	Product or intersection, or meet of two classes (math. logic) or sets (algebra) colloquially 'Cap'
∪	Sum or union or join of two classes (math. logic) or sets (algebra) colloquially 'Cup'
	Product of classes or sets between limits, used thus: $\bigcap_{n=m}^{\infty}$
	Sum of classes or sets between limits, used thus: $\bigcup_{n=m}^{\infty}$
⊼	Non-conjunction
⊎	
⊢	1) What follows is true, assertion (math. logic)
	2) Is deducible from
¬	Logical negation
∨	1) Disjunction of statements (math. logic)
	2) Sum of two sets (math. logic)
	3) Logical 'or'
∧	1) Vector product
	2) Product of two sets (math. logic)
	3) Symmetric difference of two sets (math. logic)
	4) Logical 'and'
∃	There exists
∄	There does not exist
∈	Is an element of
∉	Is not an element of
∉	Is not an element of
∀	For all
□	1) D'Alembertain operator
	2) Mean operator (finite differences)
Γ	Gamma function
∂	Partial differentiation
Δ	Increment or forward finite difference operator
∇	Nabla or del or backward finite difference operator
∇	Hamilton operator
ϑ	Curly theta
∏	Product sign
∑	Summation sign
F	Digamma function
ℵ	Aleph. The number of finite integers is $\aleph_0$ and transfinite cardinal numbers $\aleph_{1, 2, 3 ...}$
℘	Weierstrass elliptic function
&	Conjunction of statements (math. logic)
ε	Eulers sign
O	Of order, used thus: $O(x)$
o	Of lower order than, used thus: $o(x)$
f	Function of, used thus: $f(x)$
ℏ	Planck Constant over 2π
ℏ	Planck Constant over 2π
$\overline{\lim}$	Upper limit
$\underline{\lim}$	Lower limit
lim	Limits

105

∫	Integral
∮	1) Contour integral 2) Closed line integral
∯	Double contour integral
∮ (anti-clockwise)	Contour integral (anti-clockwise)
∮ (clockwise)	Contour integral (clockwise)
∮	Circulation function
⨍	Finite part integral
∫	Line integration by rectangular path around a pole
∫	Line integration by semi-circular path around a pole
∮	Line integration not including the pole
∮	Line integration including the pole
⨕	
⨖	Quaternion integral
⌐	Element of construction
⊤, ♮	Element of construction
⌒	
∠	Angle
⋆	Spherical angle
⊥	1) Orthogonal to 2) Perpendicular to
(	Parenthesis
)	Parenthesis
[	Bracket
]	Bracket
{	Brace
}	Brace
⟨	Angle bracket, colloquially 'Bra'
⟩	Angle bracket, colloquially 'Ker'
⟪	Double angle bracket
⟫	Double angle bracket
⟦	Open bracket
⟧	Open bracket
/	Italic open bracket
/	Italic open bracket
.	1) Full point 2) Scalar product
!	Factorial sign
·	Decimal point (5 unit)
·	Decimal point (9 unit)
∗	Central asterisk
∗∗	Exponent (Fortran)
′	Prime
″	Double prime
‴	Triple prime
⁗	Quadruple prime
`	Reversed prime
°	Degree
∵	Because or since
∴	Therefore, hence
:	Sign of proportion
::	Sign of proportion
∷	Geometric proportion
/	Divided by, solidus
//	Tangental to
|	1) Modulus, used thus $\|x\|$ 2) Joint denial, thus $p \mid q$ 3) Divides, thus $3 \mid 6$
∥	1) Parallel to 2) Norm of a function, used thus $\|x\|$ 3) Norm of a matrix
∦	Not parallel to
⊤	Necessarily satisfies
≡	1) Congruent to 2) Definitional identity (math. logic) 3) Identical with 4) Equivalent to (math. logic)
∤	Does not divide
#	
#	1) Is homothetically congruent to 2) Recursive function
♯	Equal or parallel

n

Newspaper Typography

Newspaper Typography

A great deal of research and development has been done since the 1930s in creating special typefaces for newspaper use. The problems of high speed printing, shrinkage and readability combined to present a challenge to the type designer.

The Mergenthaler "Legibility Group" of Ionic, Excelsior, Paragon, Opticon, Corona and Olympus, and the Intertype (now Harris) "Flexibility Group" of Ideal, Rex and Regal are the most commonly used newspaper typefaces for text. These faces are designed with a large x-height for maximum legibility and high number of characters-per-pica in order to get a high amount of content into a small amount of space.

Ionic 5 1926	E G M R a d e g n r
Excelsior 1931	E G M R a d e g n r
Opticon 1936	E G M R a d e g n r
Paragon 1935	E G M R a d e g n r
Corona 1941	E G M R a d e g n r
Times Roman 1945	E G M R a d e g n r

San Antonio Light

San Antonio Express

St. Petersburg Times

THE WALL STREET JOURNAL

The Shelton-Mason County Journal

Valley News

THE CHRISTIAN SCIENCE MONITOR

The New York Times

O

Optical Spacing

Ornaments

Outline

Optical Spacing

The essence of typography is consistent spacing. This is often difficult to achieve because of the optical illusions caused by the proximity of various letter shapes.

Letters are made of these basic shapes:

Oval   Inclined   Vertical

and the combined appearance of the spacing between letters is called "optical volume."

See **Kerning** also.

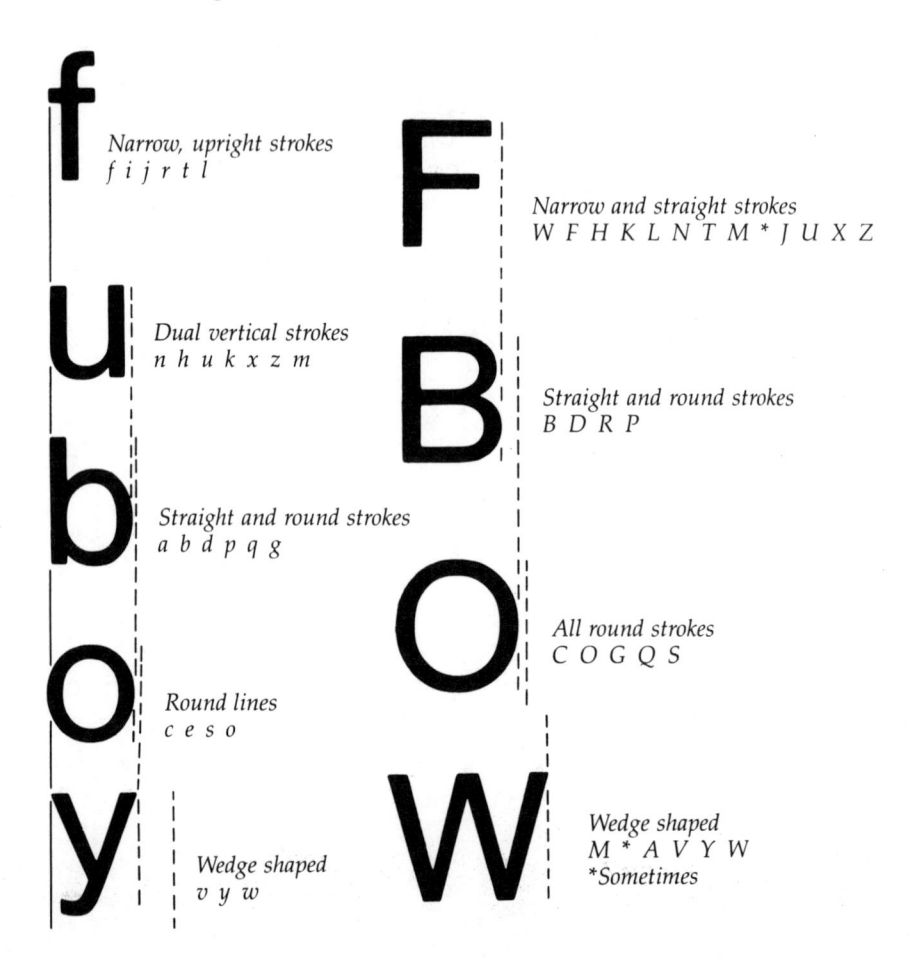

Narrow, upright strokes
f i j r t l

Narrow and straight strokes
W F H K L N T M * J U X Z

Dual vertical strokes
n h u k x z m

Straight and round strokes
B D R P

Straight and round strokes
a b d p q g

All round strokes
C O G Q S

Round lines
c e s o

Wedge shaped
M * A V Y W
Sometimes

Wedge shaped
v y w

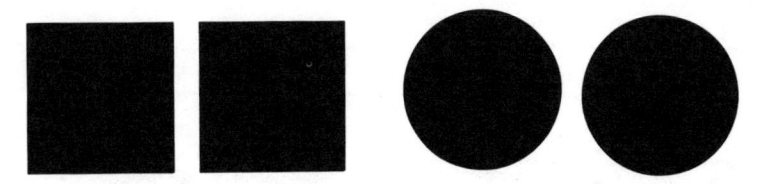

In this optical illusion, the space between the squares and circles looks different even though it is the same.

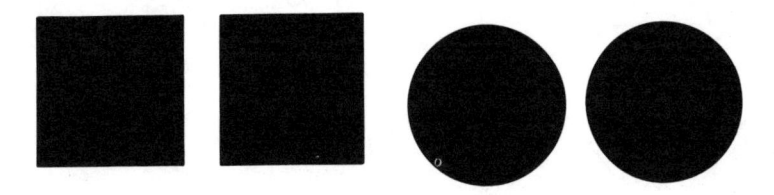

To appear "equal" the space must be modified (increased as here with the square). This is the basic principle of optical alignment—to appear proper, spacing and positioning must be modified.

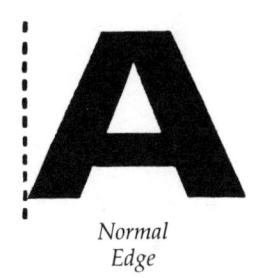

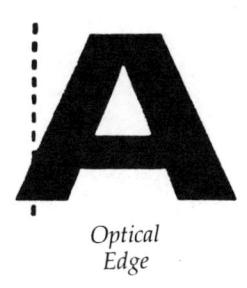

Normal
Edge

Optical
Edge

Ornaments

A symbol or decorative element. Also called "dingbats."

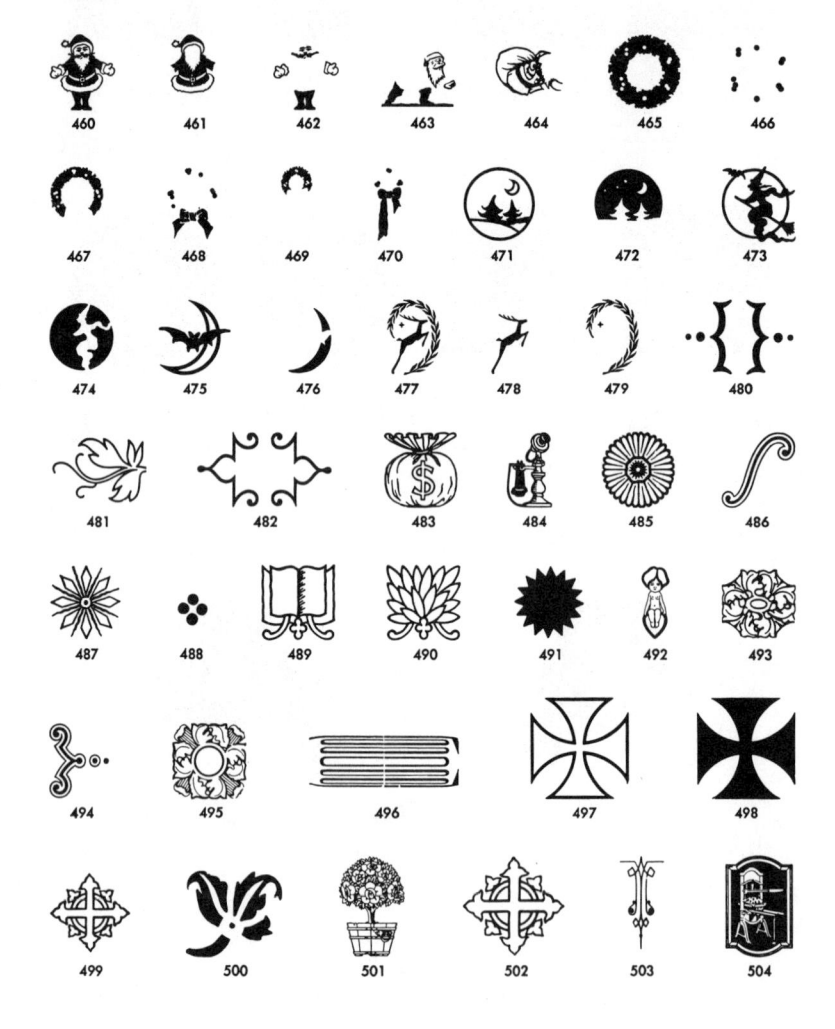

Ornaments

Outline

A typeface with no guts. Outline faces are used in display work. They lend themselves to colored or tinted layouts, allowing the type to "drop out" of the background.

ABCDEFGHIJKLMNOPQ
abcdefghijklmnopqrstu
$1234567890¢% 1234567890

FS Outline

Bookman Bold Outline

American Typewriter Outline

P

- *Paragraphs*
- *Percent*
- *Phonetics*
- *Pi*
- *Pictograph*
- *Point System*
- *Proof Marks*
- *Proportional*
- *Punctuation*

Paragraphs

Units of English compostiton; copy blocks. Paragraphs are defined by an indent at the beginning of the first line and often delineated by a short line of characters at the end. (Indents should be at least one EM and probably more.)

An alternative format involves additional line spacing (twice the visual line spacing) between paragraphs instead of the indent, or running all paragraphs together, separated by a special character, such as the paragraph symbol.

As usual, word spacing should be as close to consistent as possible and no more than three hyphens (some say two) should appear in a row.

The short line at the end of a paragraph, if less than one-third the line length is called a "widow." Sometimes a widow is considered the carryover letters of a hyphenated word (if there are no other characters on the line). If a widow is carried to the top of a column or page, it is called an "orphan." Widows and orphans should be avoided if possible.

In some few areas of the country, freeze organizers have managed to tailor the language of the petitions to include these leftist concerns—and thereby to exclude mainstream support. In the District of Columbia, for example, an initiative petition that calls for the immediate negotiation of a nuclear-weapons freeze goes on to demand the "redirection of resources to jobs and human needs." Leftists consider the juxtaposition of such issues a coup, but so far their successes have been limited. They are right in grouping economic prosperity, civil liberties, and the weapons build-up all under the same umbrella—but for the wrong reason. Money is not being diverted from social programs to the war machine, nor should it work the other way around. The Welfare/Warfare State is one cohesive unit. All money is pinched from the collective pocketbook of net taxpayers—those who pay more in taxes than they receive in benefits—which is why the left will never be able to monopolize the freeze issue. They cannot refrain from alienating the middle class, and without this taxpaying class there would be no effective mass movement at all.

The nuclear-freeze movement has simply gotten too large too fast to be molded, manipulated, or extinguished by any outside group. It has transcended the left/right political paradigm and has left both these camps to watch from the sidelines. Government leaders have been put on notice worldwide that ordinary people not only have had their fill of nuclear madness, but also no longer trust their leaders to do their thinking for them on this vital issue. Best of all, the groundswell for the freeze indicates that perhaps mankind really does have a survival instinct—and that is heartening news indeed. ∎

Normal EM paragraph indent

The list of chemical tools available to the Tree Farmer is a long one. It includes herbicides and pesticides, soil fumigants, fertilizers and tree "vitamins". What all have in common is that they must be handled, applied and stored with care.

In working with forest chemicals safely, it's important to keep them out of contact with your skin. For chemicals applied in powder form, inhaling them is another problem. Protect yourself with gloves, a long sleeve shirt or coveralls, and a hat. A face mask is important when working with dusts and sprays. Above all, *read the label completely and carefully before starting.* Don't use more than is recommended.

As with chain saws, significant hazards exist in the time frame *around* your actual work with forest chemicals. All forest chemicals take time to be absorbed by workers. If you are not wearing clothes with a residue of chemicals on them, your chance of absorbing these chemicals drops dramatically. Changing clothes after you work with chemicals may be a bother, but it is a safety must. Your chemical work clothes should not go into the regular wash, either. Clean them separately.

Always wash up between working with chemicals and meal time. Most actual poisoning cases occur as a result of kids ingesting stored chemicals rather than as a result of proper use. Never keep forest chemicals in unlabled containers that might invite juvenile tampering. Always be aware of the antidotes that are on each label. Keep chemicals under lock and key whenever possible.

Be a good example.Children will pick up your properly respectful attitude toward these substances. With the right safety steps, you can have a better Tree Farm through chemistry. Remember, a cc of prevention is worth a kilogram of cure.

Block paragraphs separated by 6-point space

Percent

The symbol representing percentage (%). When you do not have one, spell out "per cent" as two words. Italic would be preferable.

Phonetics

An alternative alphebet for pronunciation.

Ben Franklin also attempted a "phonetic" approach in 1780.

So huen sym endfiel, byi divyin kamand,
Uĥ ryiziŋ tempests fieeks e gilti land,
(Sytfi az av leet or peel Britania past,)
Kalm and siriin hi dryivs ĥi fiuriys blast;
And, pliiz'd ĥ' almyitis ardyrs tu pyrfarm,
Ryids in ĥi huyrluind and dyirekts ĥi starm.

So when some angel by divine command
With rising tempests seeks a guilty land
(Such as of late o're pale Britannia passed)
Calm and serene he drives his furious blast
And pleased the Almighty's orders to perform
Rides in the whirlwind and directs the storm

So ĥi piur limpid striim, huen faul uiĥ steens
av ryfiŋ tarents and disendiŋ reens,
Uyrks itself kliir; and az it ryns rifiyins;
Til byi digriis, ĥi flotiŋ miryr fiyins,
Riflekts üifi flaur ĥat an its bardyr groz,
And e nu hev'n in its feer byzym fioz.

So the pure limpid stream when foul with stains
Of rising torrents or descending rains
Works itself clear and as it runs refines
Till by degrees thy floating mirror shines
Reflects each flower that on its border grows
And a new heav'n in its fair bosom shows.

Pi

In phototypesetting, pi characters or pi font refers to a collection of special characters such as math or monetary symbols ⅛ ¼ ⅜ ½ ⅝ ¾ ⅞ + £ $ % ¢ $ etc. or decorative symbols ★ □ ° ■ • † etc.

If you have a special need for certain characters, most manufacturers will make a pi font to fit your need using standard characters or even develop new ones to suit you:

For instance, this font was developed for television listings:

2 3 4 5 6 7 8 9 10 11 12 13 14 15 16 17 18 19 20 21
22 23 24 25 26 27 28 29 30 31 32 33 34 35 36 37 38 39 40 41
42 43 44 45 46 47 48 49 50 51 52 53 54 55 56 57 58 59 60 61
62 63 64 65 66 67 68 69 70 71 72 73 74 75 76 77 78 79 80 81
82 83 R BW ★ DEB UT PRE MI ERE

In handset metal type, pi refers to type of one style mistakenly put in the storage drawer of another style.

When setting hand set type the composer might run across an "m" that didn't match the face he was using. He would then throw this orphan into a box of "pi" type to be sorted out later or sent back to the type foundry for credit when ordering a new font.

Primary Text Complement

ABCDEFGHIJKLMNOPQRSTUVWXYZ&
abcdefghijklmnopqrstuvwxyz
1234567890$ ([.,:;!?"%/—–-. * ½ ¼ ¾ ⅓ ⅔])

Primary Small Caps Complement

ABCDEFGHIJKLMNOPQRSTUVWXYZ
ABCDEFGHIJKLMNOPQRSTUVWXYZ&
1234567890$ ([.,:;!?"%/—–-. * ½ ¼ ¾ ⅓ ⅔])

Primary Wire Service Complement

ABCDEFGHIJKLMNOPQRSTUVWXYZ&
abcdefghijklmnopqrstuvwxyz
1234567890$ (.,:;!?"—–-. . . ½ ¼ ¾ ⅛ ⅜ ⅝ ⅞)

Supplementary Commercial Complement

+ − ± = × ÷
⅛ ⅜ ⅝ ⅞ # ° ′ ″ • £ ¢ @ † ‡ | ℓ
■ □ ◄ ► ★ ☆ • ● ® © © __ § ¶

Supplementary Advertising Display Complement

1234567890$¢ 1#°′″__
■□◀▶•●○★☆✓@®©©℗™℠

Supplementary Newspaper Display Complement

1234567890$¢ 1#°′″__
■□◀▶•●○★☆✓@®© FOR LBS ¢ ₵ ¢
lb.

Supplementary Superior and Inferior Complement

1234567890$¢ /1234567890
#|®©©℗™℠__ { } →

Supplementary Multilingual Complement

ª º °@®©©℗™℠#£¢
■□▶•__
´ ` ˆ ˇ ¨ ˜ ¯   Çç₁ß¡¿«»

Supplementary Publishing Complement

fi fl ff ffi ffl
®©℗™℠1†§#□•|__
´ ` ˆ ˇ ¨ ˜ ¯   Çç₁ß¡¿«»

Pictograph

The pictograph is a symbol representing an object. On the left is an early symbol that represents an ox; on the right is the symbol for house.

Point System

There were three principal point systems in use differing basically in decimal detail:

The American–British System, universally adopted by English-speaking countries, has for its standard of measurement the .166 pica, and the .01383 point that is one-twelfth of the pica. Thus 1000 lines of pica or 12-point matter measures 166 inches, and 1000 lines of 6-point matter measures 83 inches, and so on.

The Didot System, used in France and most countries of Continental Europe, excepting Belgium, has the cicero as its basic unit. The cicero equals 12 "corps" or .178, and the Didot "corps" or point measures exactly .01483.

The Mediaan System, used principally in Belgium, has a "corps" or point measurement of .01374. The Mediaan em or cicero measured .165. Now mostly Didot.

For general or practical measurement purposes, three decimals, or even thousandths of an inch, are deemed sufficient. If the fourth decimal equals five or more in this instance, the third is then increased by one.

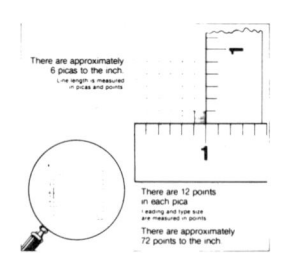

A point is also .3515 mm.

Points	American	Didot	Median
1	.01383	.01483	.01374
2	.0277	.0296	.0275
4	.0553	.0593	.0550
4¾	.0657	.0704	.0653
5	.0692	.0742	.0687
5½	.0761	.0816	.0756
6	.0830	.0890	.0824
6½	.0899	.0964	.0893
6¾	.0934	.1001	.0927
7	.0968	.1038	.0962
7½	.1037	.1112	.1031
7¾	.1072	.1149	.1065
8	.1107	.1186	.1099
8½	.1176	.1261	.1168
9	.1245	.1335	.1237
10	.1383	.1483	.1374
10½	.1452	.1557	.1443
11	.1522	.1631	.1511
11½	.1591	.1705	.1580
12	.1660	.1780	.1649
14	.1936	.2076	.1924
16	.2213	.2373	.2198
18	.2490	.2669	.2473
20	.2767	.2966	.2748
21	.2906	.3114	.2885
24	.3320	.3559	.3298
27	.3736	.4004	.3710
28	.3874	.4152	.3847
30	.4150	.4449	.4122
34	.4704	.5042	.4672
36	.4980	.5339	.4946
42	.5810	.6229	.5771
48	.6640	.7118	.6595
54	.7471	.8008	.7420
60	.8301	.8898	.8244
72	.9961	1.0678	.9893

At 30 picas or 5 inches we get 4.98"—so be careful in your calculations. It is convenient to remember 6 picas in one inch, 12 points in one pica, 72 points in one inch—but it's not quite true.

Proof Marks

Delete, Take out copy
This mark indicates that material is to be deleted. It is usually assumed that the space that results from the removal is to be closed up. In some cases the proofreader may specifically indicate "close up" by combining the delete mark with the close up marks.

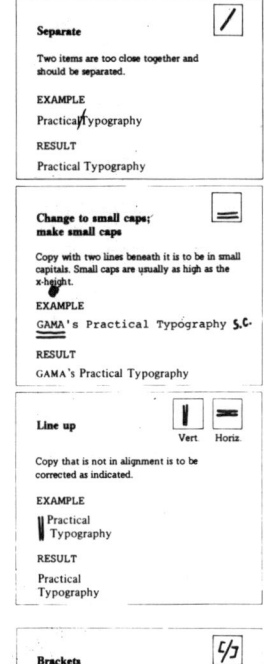

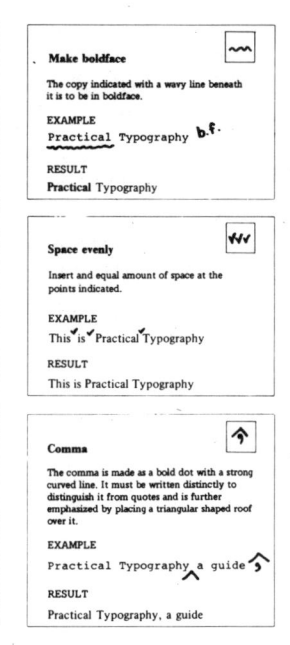

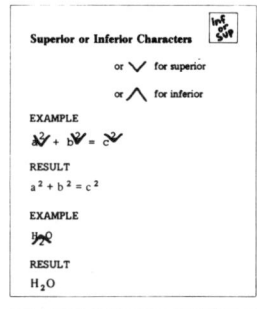

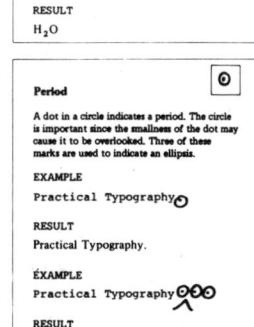

EXAMPLE
Practical Typography

RESULT
Practical Typography

Exclamation point
Also called a "bang" or "screamer". From the Latin "Io" for joy, once written as I°.

EXAMPLE
Practical Typography

RESULT
Practical Typography!

Apostrophe
Because this mark looks just like the comma, the v-shape and loop are used to distinguish it.

EXAMPLE
GAMAs Practical Typoqraphy

RESULT
GAMA's Practical Typography

Hyphen
May be indicated in any of the above ways.

EXAMPLE
Practical Typography

RESULT
Practical-Typography

Space
This is the shorthand notation for "space"—horizontal or vertical. It is usually used in conjunction with the "insert" mark or an arrow of some type.

EXAMPLE
PracticalTypography

RESULT
Practical Typography

EXAMPLE
Practical Typography
Practical Typography

RESULT
Practical Typography
Practical Typography

EXAMPLE
Practical Typography
Practical Typography
Practical Typography

RESULT
Practical Typography
Practical Typography
Practical Typography

Separate
Two items are too close together and should be separated.

EXAMPLE
Practical typography

RESULT
Practical Typography

Change to small caps; make small caps
Copy with two lines beneath it is to be in small capitals. Small caps are usually as high as the x-height.

EXAMPLE
GAMA's Practical Typography S.C.

RESULT
GAMA's Practical Typography

Line up
Vert.   Horiz.

Copy that is not in alignment is to be corrected as indicated.

EXAMPLE
Practical
Typography

RESULT
Practical
Typography

Brackets
Since these marks are somewhat similar to those for "move over" you must make them distinct so that it is known that they printout.

EXAMPLE
Practical Typography

RESULT
[Practical Typography]

Em Dash (or En Dash)
There is a distinct difference between the mark for a hyphen and a dash. Dashes are usually in EM and EN widths, although some systems make only have a 3/4 EM dash. When multiple dashes are being indicated, make sure that the number is plain.

EXAMPLE
practical typography

RESULT
practical—typography

Multiples are usually used when only the first letter of a word is printed (Mr. B——), especially if profanity is used (Go to h——), or if a statement ends abruptly (The murderer is ——).

Dashes of this length are usually used as a rule to separate heads and text, footnotes and text, or other copy. Three dashes are also used where names are repeated in a bibliography or other listing one beneath another.

OR |⊥| |EN| |3|

Make boldface
The copy indicated with a wavy line beneath it is to be in boldface.

EXAMPLE
Practical Typography b.f.

RESULT
Practical Typography

Space evenly
Insert and equal amount of space at the points indicated.

EXAMPLE
This is Practical Typography

RESULT
This is Practical Typography

Comma
The comma is made as a bold dot with a strong curved line. It must be written distinctly to distinguish it from quotes and is further emphasized by placing a triangular shaped roof over it.

EXAMPLE
Practical Typography a guide

RESULT
Practical Typography, a guide

Superior or Inferior Characters
or ∨ for superior
or ∧ for inferior

EXAMPLE
$a^2 + b^2 = c^2$

RESULT
$a^2 + b^2 = c^2$

EXAMPLE
H_2O

RESULT
H_2O

Period
A dot in a circle indicates a period. The circle is important since the smallness of the dot may cause it to be overlooked. Three of these marks are used to indicate an ellipsis.

EXAMPLE
Practical Typography⊙

RESULT
Practical Typography.

EXAMPLE
Practical Typography ⊙⊙⊙

RESULT
Practical Typography . . .

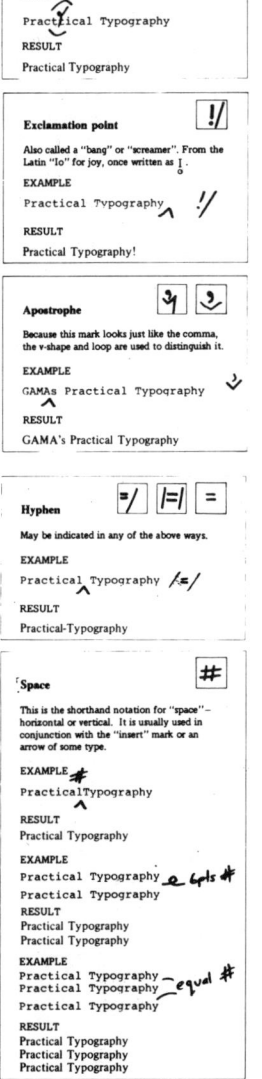

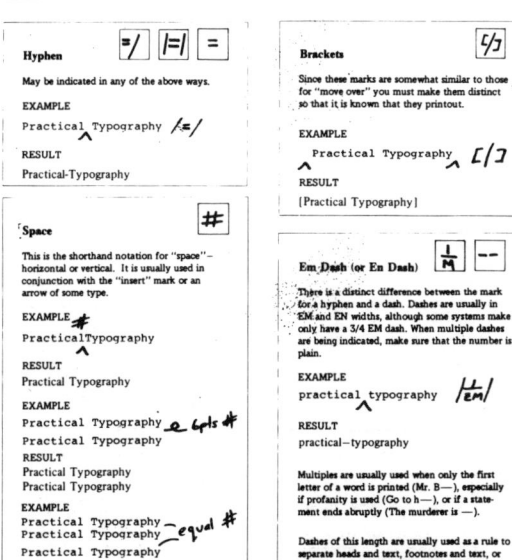

Make a new paragraph here ¶

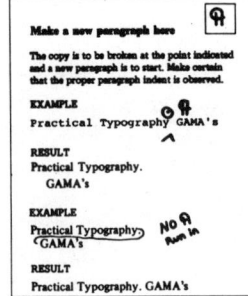

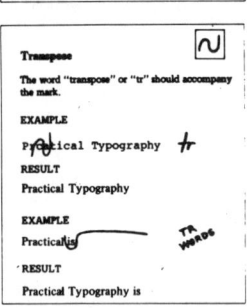

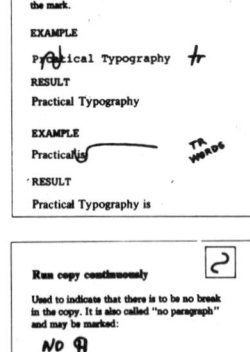

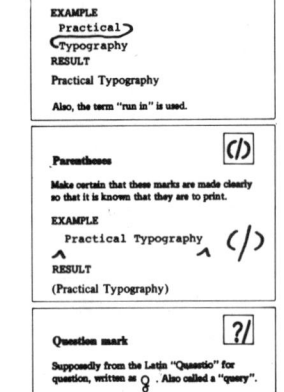

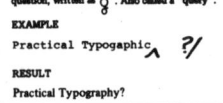

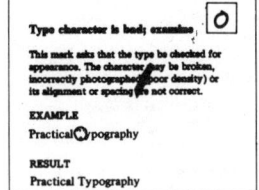

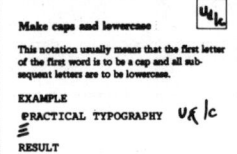

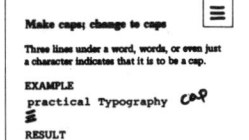

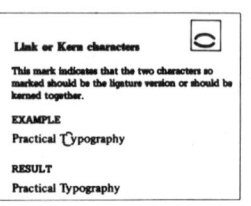

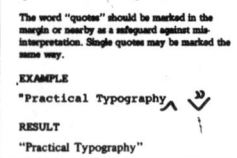

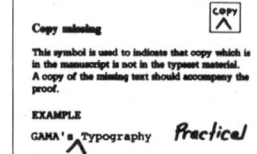

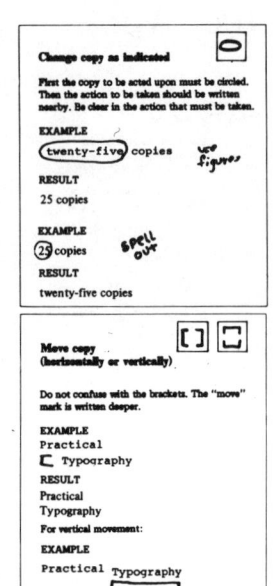

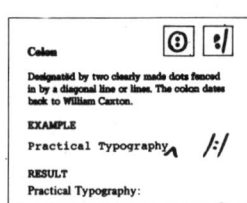

The copy is to be broken at the point indicated and a new paragraph is to start. Make certain that the proper paragraph indent is observed.

EXAMPLE
Practical Typography ⊙¶ GAMA's

RESULT
Practical Typography.
    GAMA's

EXAMPLE
Practical Typography. NO ¶
    GAMA's   Run in

RESULT
Practical Typography. GAMA's

Transpose ∽

The word "transpose" or "tr" should accompany the mark.

EXAMPLE
Pr⌒ac⌒tical Typography tr

RESULT
Practical Typography

EXAMPLE
Practical is   TR
                             WORDS

RESULT
Practical Typography is

Run copy continuously ⌒

Used to indicate that there is to be no break in the copy. It is also called "no paragraph" and may be marked:

NO ¶

EXAMPLE
Practical⌒
⌒Typography
RESULT
Practical Typography

Also, the term "run in" is used.

Parentheses (/)

Make certain that these marks are made clearly so that it is known that they are to print.

EXAMPLE
  Practical Typography   (/)
  ∧   ∧
RESULT
(Practical Typography)

Question mark ?/

Supposedly from the Latin "Quaestio" for question, written as ϙ. Also called a "query".

EXAMPLE
Practical Typographic   ?/
                   ∧
RESULT
Practical Typographic?

Type character is bad; examine O

This mark asks that the type be checked for appearance. The character may be broken, incorrectly photographed (poor density) or its alignment or spacing are not correct.

EXAMPLE
Practical Ⓣypography

RESULT
Practical Typography

Make caps and lowercase uk/lc

This notation usually means that the first letter of the first word is to be a cap and all subsequent letters are to be lowercase.

EXAMPLE
ᵖRACTICAL TYPOGRAPHY   uk/lc
         ≡
RESULT
Practical typography

Make caps; change to caps ≡

Three lines under a word, words, or even just a character indicates that it is to be a cap.

EXAMPLE
practical Typography   cap
≡
RESULT
Practical Typography

Link or Kern characters ⌒

This mark indicates that the two characters so marked should be the ligature version or should be kerned together.

EXAMPLE
Practical T⌒ypography

RESULT
Practical Typography

Quotation Marks (or Quotes) ⌄⌄ ⌃⌃

The word "quotes" should be marked in the margin or nearby as a safeguard against misinterpretation. Single quotes may be marked the same way.

EXAMPLE
ᵥPractical Typographyᵥ   ⌄⌄
RESULT
"Practical Typography"

Copy missing COPY ∧

This symbol is used to indicate that copy which is in the manuscript is not in the typeset material. A copy of the missing text should accompany the proof.

EXAMPLE
GAMA's Typography   Practical
      ∧
RESULT
GAMA's Practical Typography

Change copy as indicated ⊙

First the copy to be acted upon must be circled. Then the action to be taken should be written nearby. Be clear in the action that must be taken.

EXAMPLE
(twenty-five) copies   no figures

RESULT
25 copies

EXAMPLE
(25) copies   SPELL OUT

RESULT
twenty-five copies

Move copy [ ] ⊏⊐
(horizontally or vertically)

Do not confuse with the brackets. The "move" mark is written deeper.

EXAMPLE
Practical
⊏ Typography
RESULT
Practical
Typography
For vertical movement:

EXAMPLE
Practical Typography
         ⌐───┘
RESULT
Practical Typography

Colon ⊙ :/

Designated by two clearly made dots fenced in by a diagonal line or lines. The colon dates back to William Caxton.

EXAMPLE
Practical Typography   /:/
                    ∧
RESULT
Practical Typography:

Semicolon ;/

Again, make it distinct, and fence it in for good measure. If the dot isn't clear it may be thought to be a comma, although the comma should only be made with the triangular roof.

EXAMPLE
Practical Typography   /;/
                    ∧
RESULT
Practical Typography;

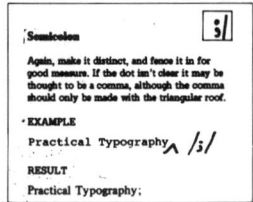

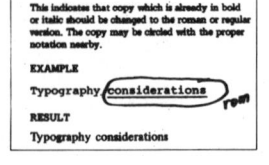

Put in Roman or Regular Font rom

This indicates that copy which is already in bold or italic should be changed to the roman or regular version. The copy may be circled with the proper notation nearby.

EXAMPLE
Typography (considerations)   rom

RESULT
Typography considerations

Proportional

Related to individual character relationships; natural widths. A narrow character has a narrow width; a wide character, a wide width, etc. Refers to character width relationships based upon character shape and typeface design.

Its opposite is *Mono Spaced* which refers to characters with the same width values; non proportional. Thus, a lowercase "i" and a lowercase "m" would have the same width, making it necessary to extend the "i" and condense the "m" to keep their spacing consistent relative to other characters.

Typewriters and line printers are the primary users of mono spaced typefaces. These are usually 10 pitch, or 10 characters to the inch (also called "pica") or 12 pitch, or 12 characters to the inch (called "elite").

Newer approaches offer finer escapement, thus allowing these faces to use a "quasi" proportional spacing approach. However, a mono spaced characher is a mono spaced character no matter how you space it.

Every typewriter character is the same width.

ABCDEFGHIJKLMNOPQRSTUVWXYZ
abcdefghijklmnopqrstuvwxyz
. , : ; ' ' ! ? - ( ) [ ] % # * /
& 1 2 3 4 5 6 7 8 9 0 $ ¢ + = @ △

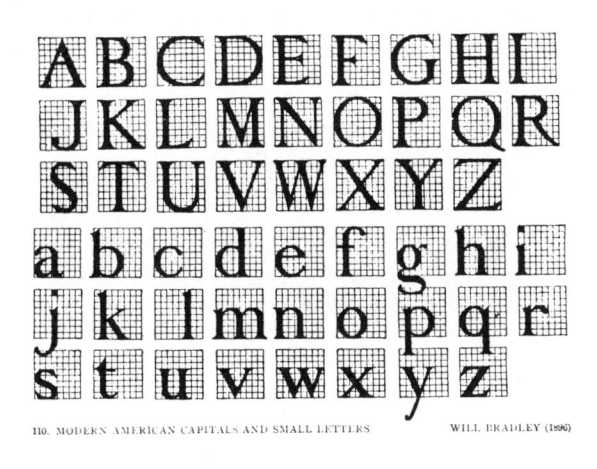

This illustration shows the relationship of typeset characters —which vary in width as the characters' design varies.

110. MODERN AMERICAN CAPITALS AND SMALL LETTERS   WILL BRADLEY (1896)

Punctuation

One of the first printers to break up text with punctuation was Aldus Manutius before 1500. The period was the full stop at the end of a sentence and the / was used as a comma, to indicate a pause in reading.

The semicolon was introduced in the late 1500s in England.

The question mark, from the Latin *quaestio* (for "what"), was shortened as Q and came to England in 1521; and the exclamation point, or "screamer" or "bang," from the Latin *io* (for "joy"), and shortened as *I* came later.

The apostrophe is used in contractions, abbreviations or to form possessives. It is not needed in plural abbreviations or numerals:

MDs

1980s

. . . but should be added to avoid ambiguity:

"Give me all the a's."

The apostrophe is *one* close quote—or the close quotes are *two* apostrophes.

Additional space at the ends of sentences is called "French Spacing" and is a very old practice, being commonplace in books up through the 19th century. It is applied in typewritten copy where two full word spaces are placed at the end of the sentence. In typesetting, a thin space in addition to the word space is the method for setting "French Spacing." The practice is difficult to implement, although computer systems will be able to automate it.

Since it was difficult to accomplish in phototypesetting, the practice was reduced; however, newer computer systems can accomplish this form of spacing automatically.

A seemingly modern practice is hanging punctuation in the margin so as to create optical justification. However, in the Gutenberg Bible, the hyphens were "hung" in the margin. So much for progress.

In quite early fonts the slash was used for the comma, or perhaps we should rather say to indicate any short pause in reading. The modern comma was introduced into England about 1521 (in roman type) and 1535 (in Blackletter). It occurs in Venetian printing before 1500.

The question mark seems to have been used in England from about 1521. The semicolon seems to have been first used in England about 1569, but was not common until 1580 or thereabouts.

The period, or full stop was commonly used *before* as well as *after* roman, and sometimes also Arabic numerals until about 1580. Thus ".xii."

' and ' were used indifferently in such abbreviations as th' or th' for "the." It may be noted that 't'is' or 't'is' (instead of "tis') was so common in the Elizabethan period that it should perhaps be regarded as normal.

Gutenberg matched the practice of the scribes of hanging the hyphens outside the justified margin for optical alignment of the text.

q

Quadding
Quotes

Quadding

In typography, another term for placement. The word comes from a short form of "quadrat," a blank cube of metal used for filling blank space in handset type. All type had to "lock up" and this necessitated that lines with only one word on them, for example, be filled with non-printing blanks. The blanks then "positioned" the type.

Linecasters mechanized the process with semi-automatic attachments that filled the blank areas of a line with metal. These "quadders" were either mechanized, electric or hydraulic. The popularity of the latter unit led to the use of the term "flush" as a verb for positioning. Today, both "flush" and "quad" are used interchangeably.

The function of quadding always takes place on the baseline between the pre-set margins.

This is Quad Left

This is Quad Right

This is Quad Center

This is *Quad Middle*

The term "quad lock" describes the function of repetitive quadding to the same position. Thus, a "quad center lock" indicates that every line (acutally every item ending with a Return) will be centered.

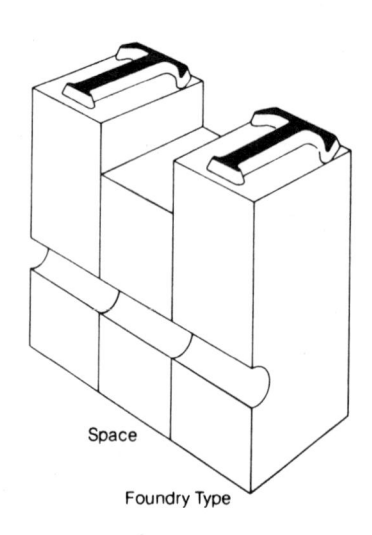

Space

Foundry Type

Quotes

Quotes are opening and closing punctuation marks to indicate verbal statements or to define or emphasize certain words. Double quotes are normally used, with single quotes used within a double quote quote, as in "Doubles on the outside, 'singles' on the inside." The close quote is an apostrophe.

Quotation marks (or quotes) were originally commas only, usually placed in the outer margin, applied by Morel of Paris in 1557. A century later they looked like the present so-called French Quotes (« ») which were placed in the center of the type body so that the same character could be used for either the open or closed position. English printers refused to use the French form and inverted the comma at the beginning and used the apostrophes at the close. Of course, they were not symmetrical. It has long been recommended that a hair space (less than a Thin Space—perhaps the equivalent of today's Unit space) is used to separate the quotes from certain letters:

'These are too close . . .
"These look better . . .
"And these don't need them . . .

"But 'Be warned to use them between multiple quotes.'"

Usually the punctuation at the end of a quote negates the need for additional space at the close.

6 9 6 9 6 9
' ' " " " "

r

Ragged

Reference Marks

Roman

Ragged

Lines of type that are not justified. The "quad" or optimum word space values should be used.

There is continuing argument about how ragged ragged should be and whether or not hyphenation should be allowed.

There are no rules—except those the "customer" makes.

The beginnings of cardiac pacing in the early 1960s were characterized by relative simplicity. The only implantable artificial pacemaker was a fixed-rate ventricular stimulator, powered by a mercury-zinc battery, whose interaction with the conduction system of the heart was easily analyzed by conventional electrocardiography. Technological improvements have changed this picture considerably, and the increasing *rate* of improvement is remarkable in itself: More than half of the significant advances in more than 2 decades occurred during the last 4 years.

Today there are roughly 500,000 patients in the United States with implanted pacemakers, or about 1 for every 460 persons (Parsonnet and Crawford 1983). Modern adaptive pacemakers, hermetically sealed in titanium cans and measuring roughly 50 g in mass, pace and sense in both atrium and ventricle; they are capable of noninvasive transcutaneous programming to millions or even trillions of possible combinations of operating-parameter values and modes. It is not surprising that microprocessors and microcomputers are playing an increasingly important role in all phases of pacemaker therapy. The state of the art in pacing is described elsewhere (Parsonnet and Bernstein 1983); in this paper we will present an overview of the use of microprocessors and microcom-

Optimum word spacing with hyphenation

The beginnings of cardiac pacing in the early 1960s were characterized by relative simplicity. The only implantable artificial pacemaker was a fixed-rate ventricular stimulator, powered by a mercury-zinc battery, whose interaction with the conduction system of the heart was easily analyzed by conventional electrocardiography. Technological improvements have changed this picture considerably, and the increasing *rate* of improvement is remarkable in itself: More than half of the significant advances in more than 2 decades occurred during the last 4 years.

Today there are roughly 500,000 patients in the United States with implanted pacemakers, or about 1 for every 460 persons (Parsonnet and Crawford 1983). Modern adaptive pacemakers, hermetically sealed in titanium cans and measuring roughly 50 g in mass, pace and sense in both atrium and ventricle; they are capable of noninvasive transcutaneous programming to millions or even trillions of possible combinations of operating-parameter values and modes. It is not surprising that microprocessors and microcomputers are playing an increasingly important role in all phases of pacemaker therapy. The state of the art in pacing is described elsewhere (Parsonnet and Bernstein 1983); in this paper we will present an overview of the use of microprocessors and microcomputers in the pacemaker pulse generators themselves, in an-

Minimum wordspacing with hyphenation

The beginnings of cardiac pacing in the early 1960s were characterized by relative simplicity. The only implantable artificial pacemaker was a fixed-rate ventricular stimulator, powered by a mercury zinc battery, whose interaction with the conduction system of the heart was easily analyzed by conventional electrocardiography. Technological improvements have changed this picture considerably, and the increasing *rate* of improvement is remarkable in itself: More than half of the significant advances in more than 2 decades occurred during the last 4 years.

Today there are roughly 500,000 patients in the United States with implanted pacemakers, or about 1 for every 460 persons (Parsonnet and Crawford 1983). Modern adaptive pacemakers, hermetically sealed in titanium cans and measuring roughly 50 g in mass, pace and sense in both atrium and ventricle; they are capable of noninvasive transcutaneous programming to millions or even trillions of possible combinations of operating-parameter values and modes. It is not surprising that microprocessors and microcomputers are playing an increasingly important role in all phases of pacemaker therapy. The state of the art in pacing is described elsewhere (Parsonnet and Bernstein 1983); in this paper we will present an overview of the use of microprocessors and microcomputers in the pacemaker pulse generators themselves, in ancillary measurement instrumentation used during implantation procedures and follow up, in making systematic choices of programmable parameter values, and in analyzing

Optimum wordspacing without hyphenation

The beginnings of cardiac pacing in the early 1960s were characterized by relative simplicity. The only implantable artificial pacemaker was a fixed-rate ventricular stimulator, powered by a mercury-zinc battery, whose interaction with the conduction system of the heart was easily analyzed by conventional electrocardiography. Technological improvements have changed this picture considerably, and the increasing *rate* of improvement is remarkable in itself: More than half of the significant advances in more than 2 decades occurred during the last 4 years.

Today there are roughly 500,000 patients in the United States with implanted pacemakers, or about 1 for every 460 persons (Parsonnet and Crawford 1983). Modern adaptive pacemakers, hermetically sealed in titanium cans and measuring roughly 50 g in mass, pace and sense in both atrium and ventricle; they are capable of noninvasive transcutaneous programming to millions or even trillions of possible combinations of operating-parameter values and modes. It is not surprising that microprocessors and microcomputers are playing an increasingly important role in all phases of pacemaker therapy. The state of the art in pacing is described elsewhere (Parsonnet and Bernstein 1983); in this paper we will present an overview of the use of microprocessors and microcomputers in the pacemaker pulse generators themselves, in ancillary measurement instrumentation used during implantation procedures and follow-up, in making systematic choices of programmable parameter values, and in analyzing

Minimum wordspacing without hyphenation

Reference Marks

Reference Marks are used instead of superior figures, usually if there are only a few footnotes. The proper sequence is:

Asterisk *
(Single) Dagger †
Double Dagger ‡
Paragraph Mark ¶
Section Mark §
Parallel Rules ‖

If more are needed, the marks start at the beginning and are doubles. At that point you should have used superior numbers.

Reference marks are placed after the text to be referenced. Usually there is no space before the reference mark, although some customers may prefer a thin space.

The Paragraph Mark and Section Mark are commonly used in legal work as in "¶5 § 351.2."

DAGGER

DOUBLE DAGGER

ASTERISK

SECTION MARK

PARAGRAPH MARK

Roman

An all-encompassing term for typefaces based upon the serif variations developed by the ancient Romans and further developed by Italian humanistic lettering. Nicolas Jenson and Aldus Manutius are credited with early uses of roman type, in place of Gothic or Blackletter type.

Today, we sometimes use the term roman to indicate the main typeface in a family of typefaces. "Times Roman," "Century Roman," etc., but this should not apply to sans serifs.

There were a number of "inspirations" for the roman typeface:

1. The first and foremost was the roman capital, as illustrated by the inscription on the Trajan column.

2. The uncial and early Blackletter variations of the Roman caps.

3. The Caroline minuscules—the "standardized" hand under Charlemagne.

4. The typefaces of Nicholas Jenson of Venice as used in *Eusebius*.

5. The faces of William Caslon, John Baskerville and Giambatista Bodoni.

RAN from the word "DECLARANDVM" in the fifth line of the Trajan Inscription

These "Trajan letter" shapes, cut into the stone panel 10 feet above the ground in the pedestal of the column, are considered the perfect roman-proportioned form, and still guide type designers. They are not all the same size because they were taken from different lines graduated in height to look the same to the viewer on the ground.

ABCDEFG
ILMNOP
QRSTVX

e e e e
g g g g
E E E E
G G G G
R R R R
Janson   Bodoni   Primer   Caledonia

Compare some roman typefaces. Note the relationship of thicks and thins.

Old Style: a characteristic style of roman typefaces typified by very little differentiation between thicks and thins, diagonal stress, capitals shorter than ascenders and serifs that are small and graceful.

Modern: a characteristic style of roman typeface typified by vertical stress, hairline serifs, and maximum contrast between thicks and thins.

Transitional: a characteristic style of roman typefaces in between Old Style and Modern, typified by sharper thick/thin contrast, sharper and thinner endings to serifs and vertical stress.

Faik   Fak

Garamond No. 3 (an old style)   *Bodoni Book (a modern style)*

Falk   Fak

Cloister (an old style)   *Baskerville (a transitional style)*

S

Sans Serif
Script
Serif
Set Width
Shaded
Small Cap
Stem
Stress
Superior/Inferior
Symmetry

Sans Serif

Characters without serifs are called *sans serif*. Supposedly, the first sans serif typeface was shown by Caslon in 1816 and picked up in 1832 by Vincent Figgins and William Thorowgood, the latter calling his face "grotesque." In the U.S., the term "gothic" was sometimes used as a synonym for sans serif. As serif type is easier to read in text; sans serif is generally more easily perceived in headlines than serif.

In the 1920s Paul Renner created a typeface called Futura, based upon geometric elements and influenced by the Bauhaus, a German school of design.

Grotesque is the *generic* term used for sans serif faces. This was, and still is the case in Germany today. The first time the word appeared was in 1832. William Thorowgood, in a supplement to his type specimen book, showed an unseriffed design which he named Grotesque.

William Caslon (the Fourth) had designed a sans serif in 1816, and when, decades later, Stephenson Blake bought him out (then Blake, Garnett & Co.) they renamed it Grotesque also. At the turn of the century, the Germans—eager to find faces more legible than Fraktur—quickly popularized the "Groteskschriften." D. Stemple AG of Frankfurt was one of the foundries that had Groteskschriften in a large number of weights and sizes, by the early nineteen hundreds.

G **g** —*Design indicative of a "Gothic"*

G **g** —*Design indicative of a "Sans Serif"*

In the periods between two world wars, England and Germany apparently did not go out of their way to share the "secrets" of their new typeface design developments with each other. The British Monotype Corporation, founded at the beginning of the Twentieth Century, had cut, as its fourth typeface, an alphabet of unseriffed capitals. In 1926 the corporation cut the 215 and 216 series.

Meanwhile, the Germans were philosophizing on letters without serifs. The principal catalyst being the Bauhaus—a training school for architects and designers which was founded in 1919 by the architect, Walter Gropius. The basic principle in all Bauhaus work was "functionalism"—simple, clinical forms without decorations. To the typographer, this meant a letter form uncluttered by serifs or variations in stroke width.

This school and its philosophies had a profound influence on the United States and Switzerland, particularly in the 1930s when the Nazi destruction of the Bauhaus drove many members of the school to find refuge in these two countries. The Swiss "Graphiker's" (graphic designer's) fine use of grotesque faces, and the excellence of the Swiss presswork, were fundamental to the success of these faces. They became even more popular after the publication of Jan Tschichold's innovative book, "Die Neue Typographie," in 1928—which was itself set in a light grotesque. In fact, grotesques were used so extensively by the Swiss (Max Bill was one of the major trendsetters) that the "New Typography" was ultimately known as "Swiss Typography."

In the 1950s, the most popular grotesques were the Monotype 215 and 216 series which virtually symbolized fine "Swiss Typography." Designers, using 215 and 216 mainly as text faces, combined them with display sizes of Neue Haas Grotesque—later developing into Helvetica.

In the U.S. these faces were called "gothic," "grotesque," and "grogothic" for many years. At present none of the terms is in common use, but may be seen in typeface names such as "News Gothic," "Trade Gothic," etc.

Faik

Spartan

GOTHIC
IS A MISLEADING NAME

NOT AN OUTGROWTH OF BLACK-LETTER

IT IS A RUDE IMITATION OF THE EARLIEST FORMS OF ROMAN LETTER CUT IN STONE

THIS FACE OF TYPE

IS KNOWN IN GREAT BRITAIN AS

GROTESQUE

IT IS THE SIMPLEST FORM OF LETTER, WITH STROKES NEARLY UNIFORM IN THEIR THICKNESS, AND WITHOUT SERIFS, FOR WHICH REASON IT IS SOMETIMES CALLED

SANS-SERIF

In 1890, DeVinne tried to explain "Gothic," "Grotesque" and "Sans Serif."

141

Script

Typefaces designed with connecting characters in imitation of fine handwriting. Should never be used in all caps. There are various levels of script ranging from informal styles (Brush) to Spencerian styles. All are calligraphic in nature.

ABCDEFGHIJKLMN OPQRSTUVWXYZ &

abcdefghijklmnopqrstuvwxyz 1234567890(.,:;!? '' — /$-%)

August Casual (823)
Brush (984)
Cascade (596)
Dom Casual (822)
Discus (1001)
Gando Ronde (597)
Gavotte Script (335)
Kaufmann (445)
Kaufmann Bold (446)
Linoscript (598)
Lotus Script (857)
Medici (599)
Mistral (1067)
Neris Script (600)
Nuptial Script (601)
Park Avenue (602)
Present (897)
Shelley Allegro (604)
Shelley Andante (603)
Shelley Volante (605)
Snell Roundhand (623)
Snell Roundhand Bold (624)
Snell Roundhand Black (625)
Stuyvesant Script (856)
Venture (607)

Serif

Serif is an all-inclusive term for characters that have a line crossing the free end of a stroke. It is said that the Romans invented the serif as a solution to the technical problem of getting a chisel to cut a neat, clean end to a character.

Later it became an emulation of handwriting with flat "pens" that produced thick and thin curves.

Certainly, serif characters help reading by providing a horizontal guideline for the eye to "tie" the letters of a word together. It is generally better to use serif faces when typesetting long stretches of copy such as books with a few illustrations since serif faces cause less fatigue on the eyes.

Early typefaces were imitations of handwriting, and the scribes or "copyists" ended their characters with graceful arcs and curves.

Half serifs on horizontal arms are sometimes called "beaks," and serifs at the end of arcs are called "barbs."

The most common types of serifs are:

Thin (or Hairline) Serifs

Square (or Slab) Serifs

Round Serifs

Cupped Serifs

Here are some examples of serifs:

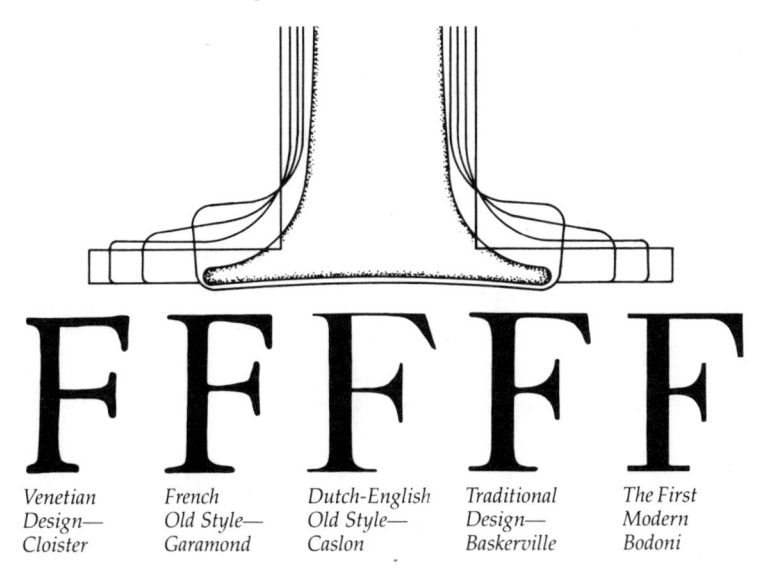

F F F F F

Venetian Design— Cloister
French Old Style— Garamond
Dutch-English Old Style— Caslon
Traditional Design— Baskerville
The First Modern Bodoni

Set Width

A concept applied to character width, which is no longer universally applicable. You know that all characters of a typeface can be output in a particular point size. The width of the characters increases as the size does; and the widths are programmed to relate to the size. Thus, a 9-point font has widths that are 9-set (width); 18-point is 18-set. Some faces are designed somewhat narrower and you might have 9-point on 8.5-set.

Some typesetters allow you to change the set size by machine command. Actually what changes is the space on either side of the character (its total width), but the acutal width of the character itself does not change. Thus, 9-point, 8-set actually "tightens" the character spacing.

More appropriately, negative letterspacing commands, in either actual or relative unit values, are used to tighten spacing, or reduce white space.

The concept of set is different as practiced by digitized typesetters. Here, because characters are made up of dots, one can actually condense the actual width of a character electronically. A 9-point character can be output at various levels of condensation (or expansion). But, here again, the use of the word "set" is not accurate. The characters are being condensed (or expanded) in programmable movements (12% units or 1% units, for example).

Also see **Letterspacing** for a better understanding of character width modification.

A "unit" is not a constant. It gets bigger or smaller as the point size changes.

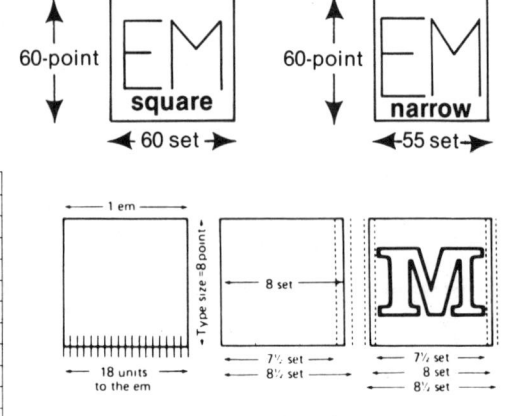

3 Units	4 Units	5 Units	6 Units	7 Units	8 Units	9 Units
i	f	a	b P	B	w V	m
j	r	c	d S	C	A X	M
l	s	e	h *	E	D Y	W
.	t	g	k †	F	G &	
,	l	v	n $	L	H %	
:	;	z	o +	T	K @	
;	)	J	p =	Z	N –	
'	(	?	q]		O ¾	
`	!	]	u		Q ½	
-		/	x		R ¼	
			y		U	
			All numbers			

A 9-unit system of width allocation.

60-point EM **square** ◄ 60 set ►

60-point EM **narrow** ◄ 55 set ►

1 em / 18 units to the em / Type size =8point / 8 set / 7½ set / 8½ set / 7½ set / 8 set / 8½ set

Only the side space changes.

144

Shaded

A typeface designed with a third dimension, a drop shadow or a drop outline. Lends itself to 2-color display applications.

AÆBCDEFG
HIJKLMNOP
QRSTUVWXY
Z&(.',:;"")?!.$
1234567890
¢/£% (WV)

Sans Serif Shaded

AÅÄ
ÆBCÇDEFG
HIJKLMN
OÖØŒPQ
RSTUVW
XYZ&(.',:;"")?
!¿aåäæbcç
defghijkl
mnoøöœpq
rstuvwxyz
ß$1234567
890¢/.‰ (CMM) (WV)

Belwe Bold Shaded Design

Small Cap

Capital letters designed to match the x-height of a particular typeface and size:

ABCDEFGHIJKLMNOPQRSTUVWXYZ&
abcdefghijklmnopqrstuvwxyz   fiflffffiffl
$1234567890   .,-'':;!?

ABCDEFGHIJKLMNOPQRSTUVWXYZ& *Small Caps*
ABCDEFGHIJKLMNOPQRSTUVWXYZ&
abcdefghijklmnopqrstuvwxyz   fiflffffiffl
$1234567890   :;!?

Since many fonts today do not have small caps, they are "manufactured" by reducing the point size by two sizes (or 80%), setting capital letters, and then returning to the original size. Of course, these are not true small caps, however, they may be lighter than the caps and look out of place. "True-cut" small caps are usually equal to the normal cap width, thus they are slightly expanded. That's because they were on the same hot metal matrix as the cap character and thus had to have the same width as the wider character. Digitized typesetting devices have an advantage in being able to reduce size in smaller increments and to electronically expand characters to form small caps.

Words in text that are specified as all caps could look better (in terms of typographic color of the page) in small caps. This is also true of lining figures—they look best slightly smaller. Old Style figures look best with small caps.

Also, the use of full cap initial letters with small cap is not advised. All small caps is better. Small caps should be used for appreviations of awards, decorations, honors, titles, etc., following a person's name.

MANY TIMES IT IS DESIRED TO SET MATTER IN MEASURES SO NARROW THAT IT IS IMPOSSIBLE TO Avoid Either Wide Spacing Between The Words Or Spacing between letters, *and often both*. **Again the ability of the Monotype to vary the width of the body on which** *each character* **is cast comes into play; in such $1234567890**

Stem

The main vertical stroke or principal stroke in an oblique character or face is the dominant element in most characters. Elements which are perpendicular to the stem or connected to it or other main parts of the letter are:

Arm—Horizontal stroke starting from stem, as in the cap E or F.

Bar—An arm connected on both sides, as in the cap H.

Crossbar—Horizontal stroke which crosses through the stem as in the lowercase t. The cap T stroke is more accurately two arms.

Ear—Short stroke extending from bowl of lowercase g, stem of lowercase r.

Tail—A downward sloping short stroke, ending free.

The outer portion of arms and serifs of the letters E, F, G, T, and Z is called a *Beak*.

Any curved stroke that is *not* a bowl, is an arc. A "spine" is the main curved (arc) section of the letter S.

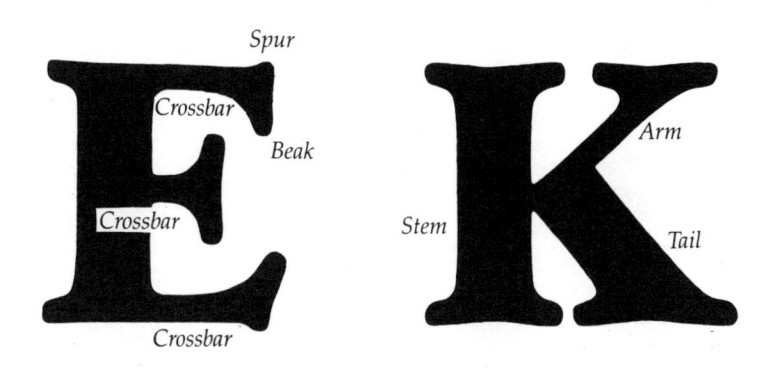

Stress

The gradation in curved strokes from thick to thin.

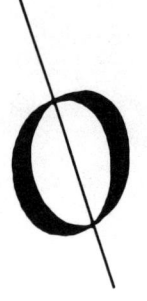

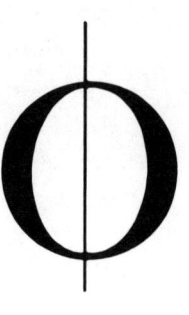

Superior/Inferior

Superior or Inferior characters are usually in a smaller point size than the typeface in use and positioned above or below the baseline. They are also called Subscripts (Inferior) and Superscripts (Superior). They are used for:

1. Chemical equations
2. Math
3. Footnote references

They are most often numerals, but alphebetic characters are sometimes used as well.

Superior and Inferiors can be "manufactured" by changing to a smaller size and advancing or reversing line spacing (if this capability is available) for positioning.

Correct superior position	H^{AAA}
Aligned at top of cap	H^{BBB}
Centered on cap height	H^{CCC}
Base aligned	H$_{DDD}$
Correct inferior position	H$_{EEE}$
Below baseline	H$_{FFF}$

Symmetry

A predictable pattern or arrangement. Symmetry is order, balance—all elements in harmony.

Asymmetry is the opposite, with no predictable pattern.

t

| *Tabular* |
| *Terminal* |
| *Trap* |
| *Type Series* |
| *Type Size* |

Tabular

Tabular compostion is essentially vertical alignment within multiple columns.

A combination of en spaces (figure spaces) and thin spaces are used to line up tabular material.

In word processing and computer systems, the same thing is accomplished by automatic decimal alignment.

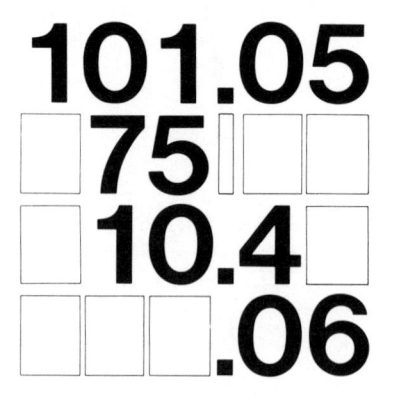

101.05
☐75☐☐
☐10.4☐
☐☐.06

A combination of en spaces (figure spaces) and thin spaces are used to line up tabular material.

Terminal

This is a free ending stroke with a special treatment:
- *Acute*—angle of acute accent.
- *Concave*—Rounded, out.
- *Convex*—Rounded, in.
- *Flared*—Extended.
- *Grave*—At angle of grave accent.
- *Hook*—Looped.
- *Pointed*—To a point.
- *Sheared*—Sliced off.
- *Straight*—Even.
- *Tapered*—Graduated.

Another form of terminal is the "finial" which may be an alternative ending. There are several forms:
- *beak*—Most often a half serif.
- *Barb*—At end of an arc.
- *Swash*—Florished.

Ball terminal **y**

Trap

A compensating indentation cut into the intersection of strokes on a letter. Particularly in phototypesetting and especially on bold faces, the problem of "bleed" arises frequently, due to changes in focus, light exposure intensity and even bleed of ink in printing. If any of these factors are off, the intersection of stokes on the character will look rounded and not "sharp" in the finished piece.

To compensate for this, "traps" are cut in these problem areas (see illustration). When finally printed, photographic and ink bleed bring the intersection out to where it optically belongs.

Often, a character must be redesigned several times before the ideal trap for that character is found.

A problem with traps is that they often show up when typesetting in large point sizes.

→
Art for text sizes 4 to 14 point

AA

←
Art for display sizes 15 to 18 point

Type Series

A series is the range of sizes of a particular font in a particular typeface:

Type family: Helvetica.

Typeface: Helvetica Light Condensed (Weight and Width).

Type size: 10-point Helvetica Light Condensed.

Type font: 10-point Helvetica Light Condensed with a job layout of 96 characters.

Type series: 6 to 18-point Helvetica Light Condensed with a job layout of 96 characters.

There are several variations in the output of type:

1. *Master.* The master image may be modified for the technical considerations of the device.

2. *Outputting.* The output device, in the process of outputting, may create variation.

3. *Processing.* The development of the image by photographic means or the use of newer technologies can affect the resultant image.

4. *Operator Control.* Deliberate changes in density, weight, width, size, or position by the operator.

It is no wonder that type cannot be matched precisely.

Type Size

The basic unit of measurement in typography is the *point*. All other dimensions and terms used in printing derive from this one unique measurement. The *point* is used to describe the differences in size between typefaces, line spacing, and other elements of composition, but it also leads to great confusion. The growth of printing technology has fostered several incompatible systems for measuring type, all based on the *point* but none having a *point* of equal size.

In North America and Britain the point is approximately $1/72$ of an inch (.351 mm) and is called the *pica point*. In Europe the point is a little bigger (.376 mm) and is called the *Didot point*. These two units can be related in the proportion 7:5.5.

In both systems, points have always been used to describe the length of one metal chunk of type. A 72-point H, in metal type, is a character cast onto the top of a metal block; the block carries the letter through all the printing operations and the block's top surface is itself exactly 72 points (or one inch) in height. The actual impression or image height of the H, when printed on paper, will be smaller than the overall size of the metal. Traditionally, the point size refers to a specific dimension of the metal and *not* to the image height. This discrepancy is necessary because of the *ascenders* and *descenders*. If the type is to line up squarely and securely, each character must be cast onto oversize metal blocks which are large enough to allow for these extremes of projection above and below the baseline. Thus, all the metal blocks end up being equal in height, and this height is what determines the point size of the typeface.

For centuries, there was no system for comparing (in the same units) two typefaces of different size. Each individual size had a name at one time, not a number (Diamond, Brevier, Pica, Great Primer, etc.), but could not be related quantitatively to faces just above and below it in size. Finally, in the late 1800s, the industry adopted the point system which had been developed in France a century earlier by Pierre Fournier. The point system has resulted in better descriptions of metal size and of the amount of vertical spacing between lines of type, but has left other matters unresolved. Point size is only an expression of the distance from ascender to descender (plus a little bit of space above and below for the metal *shoulder*) and, as such, cannot describe the proportional relationship of a typeface's x-height to its ascenders and descenders. If one chooses two dissimilar 60-point faces (e.g. Helvetica vs. Garamond), they will appear on the page very differently. Since it is the x-height of the typeface which most directly influences its appearance on the page, a 60-point face with short ascenders and descenders will have a much greater visual impact. Both of the faces below are 60-point, yet notice how much larger the Helvetica seems by virtue of its x-height.

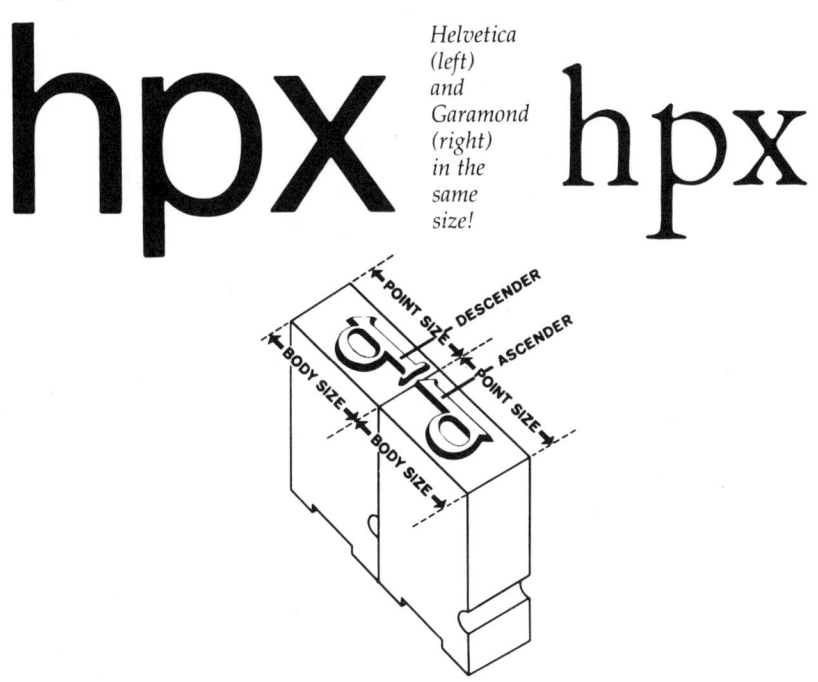

hpx

Helvetica (left) and Garamond (right) in the same size!

hpx

The usefulness of the point in describing line spacing and the like cannot be denied. When one is discussing very small type, it is preferable to deal in round numbers (rather than fractions of inches or millimeters). Typefaces now can come in pica points, or in Didot points. In the United States we used only pica points until 1960 or so, with the expection of certain faces such as Bauer Bodoni and the original Helveticas (which had been around—in Didot points—for considerably longer). Then typefaces from Europe began to be imported for use in Linotype and Monotype systems, and these faces were cut in Didot points. The result has been a far greater selection of typefaces, but even further complication in describing the height of a specific letter. A font of "24-point" letters may have been adapted from hot type 24 *pica* points high, hot type 24 *Didot* points high, or from photolettering which itself has some tenuous point designation. It may even have been designed originally for phototype, in which case the capital letters might be 24 points high (pica *or* Didot). The traditional point measurements associated with hot type are a hindrance in the world of phototype. Much of the type composed these days does not use metal slugs, but appears directly on a sheet of paper of film. We could change to a system using actual letter image heights with very little difficulty. This would be a much more logical way to exploit the special attributes of phototype; the height of a capital H can simply be expressed in points or, perhaps, millimeters.

Originally, type size referred to the individual piece of metal that held each character. The character and linecasters did not change this approach. For many years type size was a constant measurement and only the x-height varied. Since there were few sizes cast for faces at that time, it was not a difficult task to learn to identify sizes on sight. The advent of photographic typesetting changed all that.

There were two divergent approaches. The first was that of *photolettering* which referred to headline and display work. The master size on the photo matrix was usually one inch (72-point) and all enlargements and reductions modified this basic size. Thus, the concept of standard type sizes was lost since one could specify and size necessary to fit a layout, and the past increments of 6, 7, 8, etc. were meaningless in the new world of photolettering.

Then came *phototypesetting* or better, *phototextsetting*, and three approaches were applied for type sizing.

1. Each photo matrix had a different master size and characters were photographed 1:1.

2. The photo matrix had one master size, 8-point for example, and lenses enlarged or reduced the character image.

3. There were "ranges" or master sizes so that a photo matrix with the 8-point master would only be used for enlargement up to 12-point, and another photo matrix would have a master size of 12-point for enlargement up to 18-point, for example.

Some suppliers made their master sizes all the same size and worked from constant sized artwork. Thus, all typefaces would be 7" and reduced to the 8-point master size. In many cases this effectively eliminated the x-height variability. All sizes were then simple enlargements and reductions. And all sizes in all faces were then the same.

Other suppliers may have used a constant sized artwork but they varied the acutal character size thereon in in order to more accurately reflect the typeface's hot metal x-height.

In newer digitized typesetting the image is not a photographic master. It is made up of thousands of dots, overlapped to create lines (called rasters). Thus, the number of type sizes is increasing.

1. Hot metal limited the number of type sizes because of the sheer weight of carrying a face in too many sizes.

2. Size-for-size photo matrices also limited the number of sizes available since the typesetting device could not hold too many masters to begin with.

3. The lens machines were at first limited by the number of lenses that could fit in the turret but the zoom lens machines can give an extended range.

4. Digitized typesetters create sizes electronicaly and can thus give us an almost infinite size range.

To summarize:

1. Hot metal—15 to 20 sizes from 6 to 72 point.
2. Photo, size for size—20 to 25 sizes, 6 to 72 point.
3. Photo, lens turret—12 to 20 sizes, 5½ to 72 point.
4. Photo, zoom lens—50 to 140 sizes, 51/2 to 74 point.
5. Digital—200 to 700 sizes, 5 to 120 point.

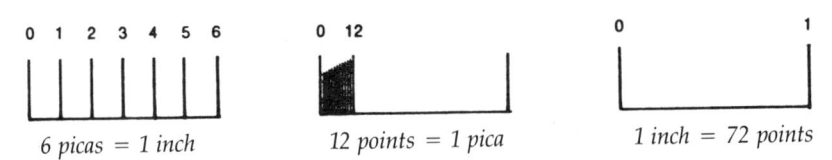

6 picas = 1 inch

12 points = 1 pica

1 inch = 72 points

But that is really not the truth. You see one point = .01383", thus one inch is 72 × .01383 or .996" (acutally .99576"). Now, this means that 360 points is not really 5 inches (5 × 72); it is 4.978". But everyone rounds out, so it probably does no real harm.

1 point = .01383"
1 inch = .996" or 72 points
1 pica = 12 points or .166"

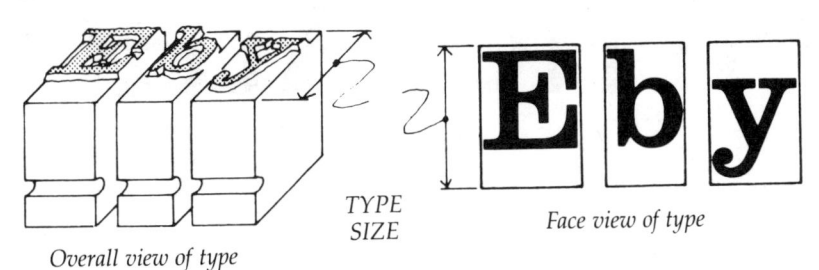

TYPE SIZE

Face view of type

Overall view of type

THERE WAS A TIME WHEN TYPESETTING W
There was a time when typesetting was only the
process of assembling individual pieces of type by
hand. Gutenberg printed his Bible from movable
type in the middle of the Fifteenth Century in this

Helvetica

**THERE WAS A TIME WHEN TYPESETTING W
There was a time when typesetting was only the
process of assembling individual pieces of type by
hand. Gutenberg printed his Bible from movable
type in the middle of the Fifteenth Century in this**

Times Roman

THERE WAS A TIME WHEN TYPESETTING WA
There was a time when typesetting was only the process
of assembling individual pieces of type by hand. Gutenberg printed his Bible from movable type in the middle of
the Fifteenth Century in this way. The first major ad-

Souvenir

THERE WAS A TIME WHEN TYPESETTING WAS
There was a time when typesetting was only the process of
assembling individual pieces of type by hand. Gutenberg
printed his Bible from movable type in the middle of the
Fifteenth Century in this way. T! first major advance in

Garamond

*Each of these settings is 11 on 11; note that the smaller
x-height faces have "build-in" leading.*

At ad At ad

Times Roman   *Garamond*

At ad At ad

Souvenir   *Helvetica*

Each of these type samples is 72 point—but notice that there are visual differences.

u

| *Uncial* |
| *Unit System* |

Uncial

From the Latin word for crooked, "uncus," an uncial was a capital letter that rounded the straight lines. Uncials were essentially "biform" characters making the transition from caps to lowercase as scribes tried to write faster and faster.

Phoenician	⊿ᕥገ⊐ ⴺ ᕼ⋎ⱳ
Greek	ΑΒΓΔΕΗΚ
Roman	ABCDEHKM
Uncial	abcdehkm
Half Uncial	abcdehkm
Caroline	Abcdefghikm
Caroline Minuscule	abcdefghikm
Gothic	abcdefghiklmno
Blackletter	abcdefghiklm
Libra	aBCDefGhijklmn

Unit System

It all started when Tolbert Lanston invented the Monotype. He wanted to separate the functions of input and output and needed a method that would let the operator know when to end a line for justification. Arithmetic was the best idea: he would add up character widths. To store the widths of every character in *every* point size of *every* face would have been prohibitive. So he created *relative* widths.

In any typeface all characters are proportional to one another . . . and from point size to point size that proportionality remains the same. Thus, if I describe the width of every character as a multiple of some value, then those numerical realtionships will still be valid no matter what the size is.

An "a" in 9 point might be $8/18$ths; the "a" in 72 points is also $8/18$ths. You differentiate the real width that these characters occupy by multiplying the realtive values by the point size:

9 point × 8 unit "a" = 72

72 point × 8 unit "a" = 576

Thus, one set of values serves for all sizes of a particular typeface. Lanston's base was 18 and that served phototypesetting for many years. In order to speed up film font manufacture, suppliers moved to 36, 54, 72 and more unit systems.

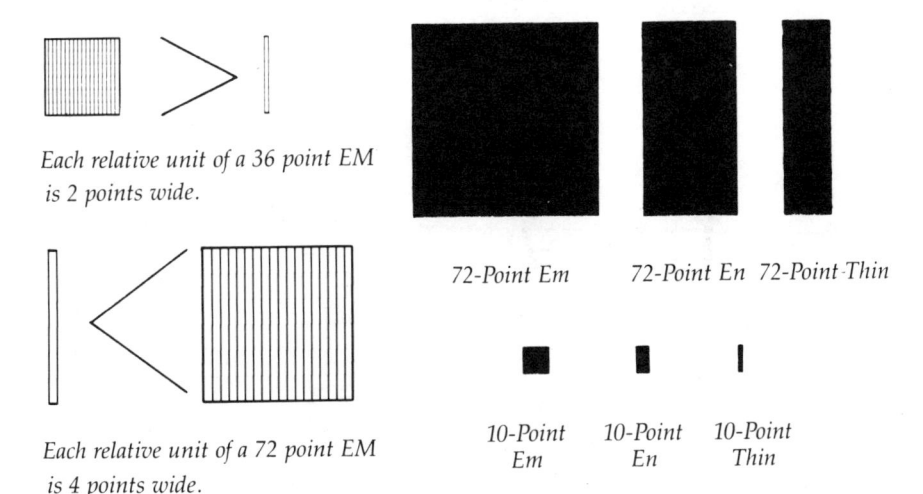

Each relative unit of a 36 point EM is 2 points wide.

Each relative unit of a 72 point EM is 4 points wide.

72-Point Em   72-Point En   72-Point Thin

10-Point Em   10-Point En   10-Point Thin

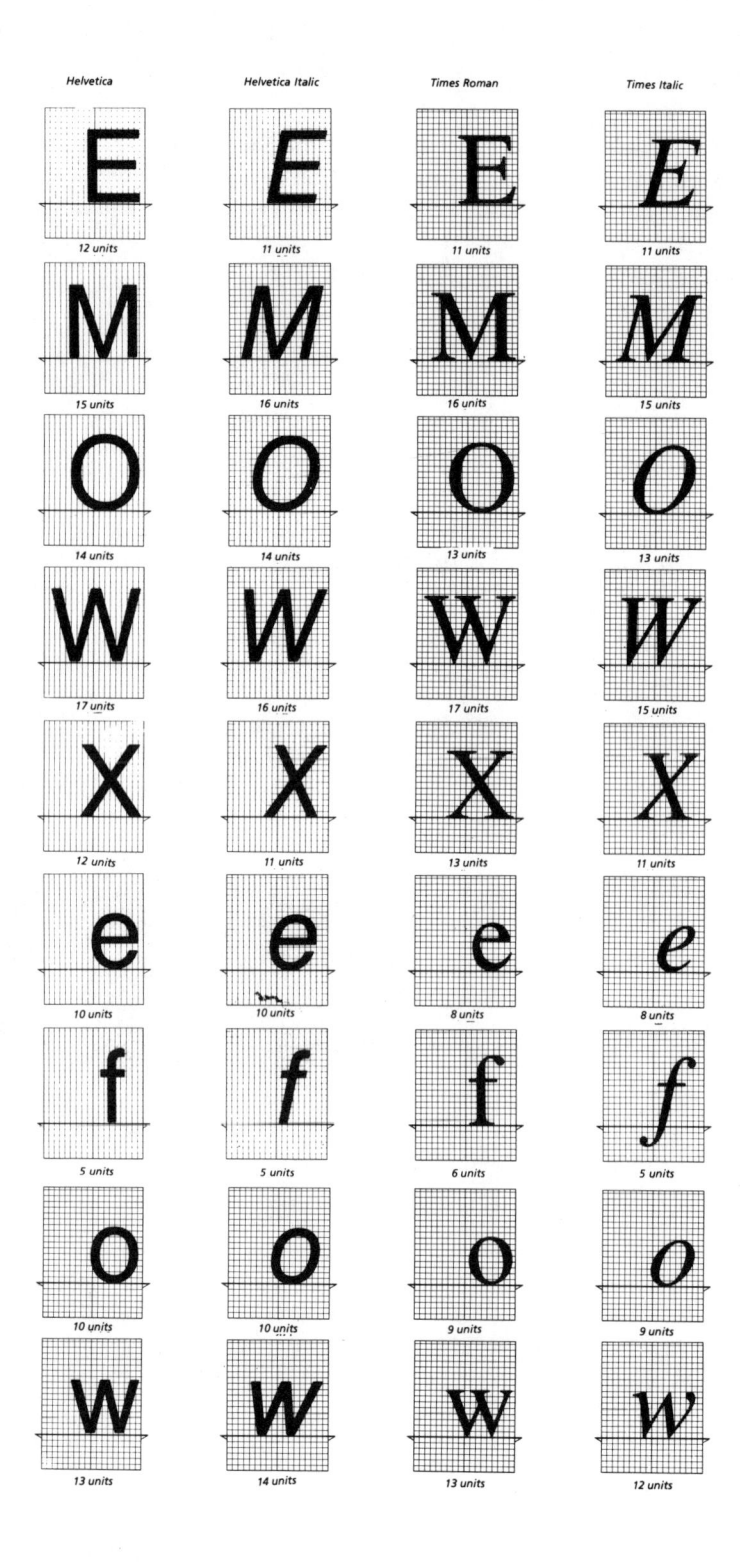

Helvetica	Helvetica Italic	Times Roman	Times Italic
E	E	E	E
12 units	11 units	11 units	11 units
M	M	M	M
15 units	16 units	16 units	15 units
O	O	O	O
14 units	14 units	13 units	13 units
W	W	W	W
17 units	16 units	17 units	15 units
X	X	X	X
12 units	11 units	13 units	11 units
e	e	e	e
10 units	10 units	8 units	8 units
f	f	f	f
5 units	5 units	6 units	5 units
o	o	o	o
10 units	10 units	9 units	9 units
w	w	w	w
13 units	14 units	13 units	12 units

18-Unit

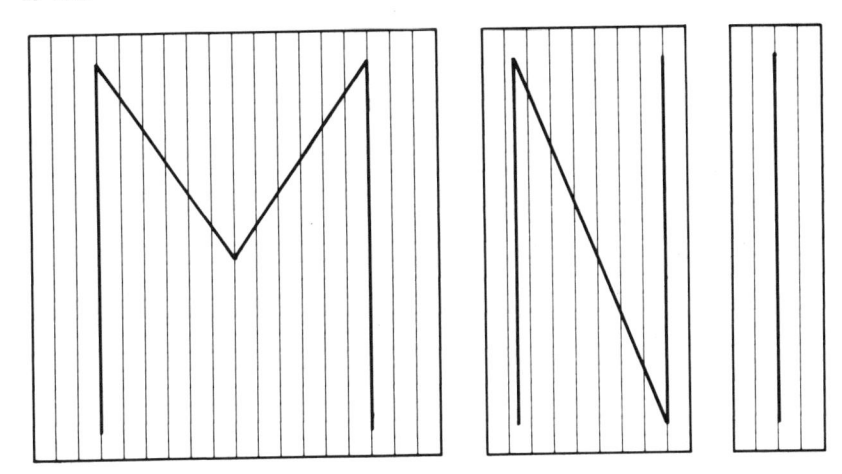

All characters have widths that are in units of 1/18th wide.

A 54-unit system has smaller increments—allowing finer spacing.

54-Unit

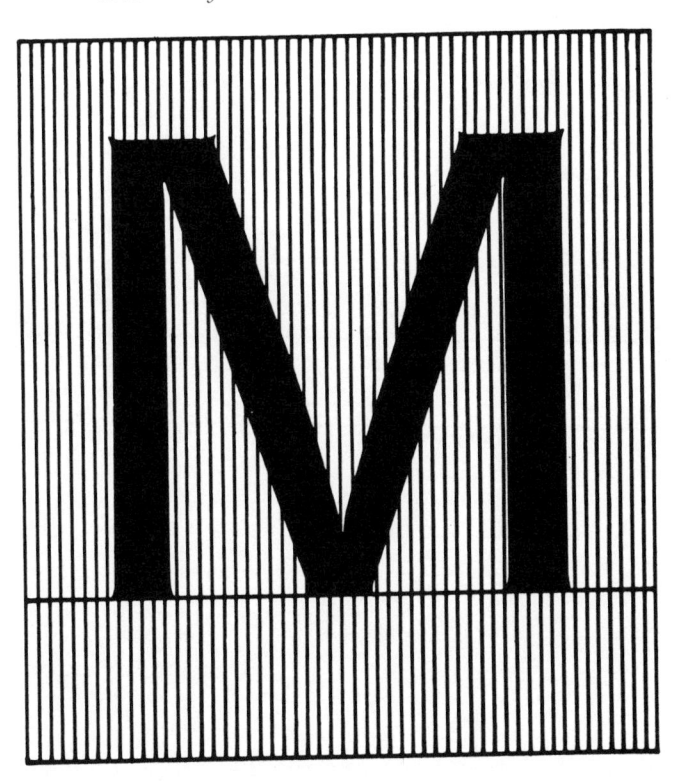

V

Vertical Setting

Vertical Setting

Setting type with letters over and under one another.

1. Vertical Stacking

    T
    Y
    P
    E

2. Standard book edge

    TYPE

Also see **Alignment.**

W

Weight
Word Space

Weight

Refers to the lightness or darkness in print of a particular typeface based upon its design and thickness of line. We call this a variation of weight.

The standard gradations of weight are: extra-light, light, semi-light, medium, semi-bold, bold, extra-bold and ultra-bold (also called "black"). (Extremely light typefaces are often called "hairline.")

Then, medium, semi-bold (or demi-bold), bold, extra-bold and ultra-bold. The last two are sometimes called "Heavy" or "Black." There is no standardization of these terms: Helvetica Medium may be the same weight as a Universe Bold. In phototypesetting, one must be *very* careful when determining if a face is light or regular, medium or bold.

In markup, bold is indicated by a wavy line. Most typefaces have companion bold versions.

Due to variables such as the condition of processor chemicals, length of time since processing the galley (fading), and density setting on the typesetting machine itself, differences in weight may be artificially created.

When trying to identify the typeface on a previously printed piece you must consider thickness or density of the ink, the amount of bleed, and the number of photographic steps that the image went through.

A bold lead-in, where the first word of a paragraph is bold, should be in the same face and size as the text. If not, at least base-align the copy.

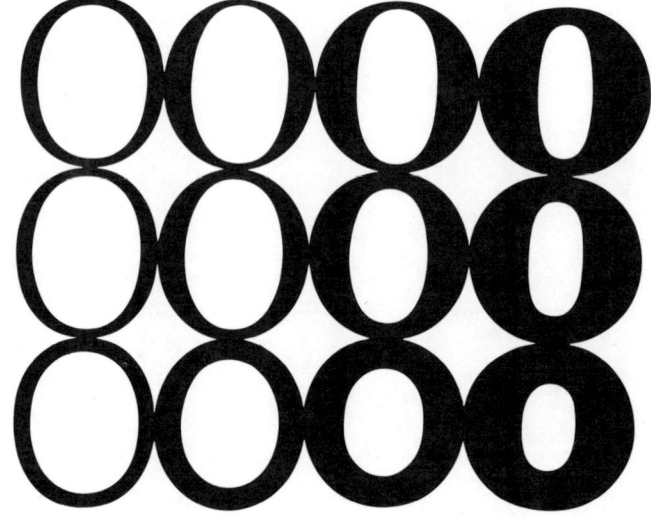

Word Space

Unlike a typewriter which has word spaces of the same width, the word space in typography is *variable*—it expands or contracts based upon the length of line, number of characters on the line and the number of word spaces on the line.

This is quite important. The justification process can only work with *variable* word spaces, and practitioners must realize that a word space cannot be used as an indent or in other places where a *fixed* constant width space is required (see **Fixed Space**).

Typists who are accustomed to keying two word spaces at the end of a sentence will find that this practice is not applicable in automated typography (see **Punctuation—French Spacing**).

Word spaces are usually within certain ranges—minimum, optimum, maximum—and these can be tailored by users in many cases to their own taste. The *minimum* word space is the value below which the space will not go. This would reduce the likelihood that a line would be set completely tight with no discernable word spaces. The *maximum* is the widest value you would allow and usually this is the threshold point where automatic letterspacing might be employed (if allowable). The *optimum* is the value that you would like most often for good, even spacing (this is just about the width of the lowercase i of the font and size).

In ragged setting or quadded lines the optimum value is usualy used throughout.

Less word space, or even kerned word spaces, often looks better after commas, periods, apostrophes or quotes.

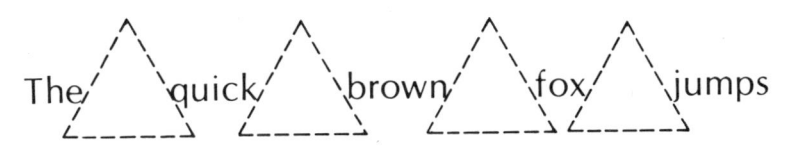

The quick brown fox jumps

(Partially justified)

Think of word spaces as expandable wedges.

em	*The space between words*
en	*The space between words*
thin	*The space between words*
thin kern 2	*The space between words*
no space	*Thespacebetweenwords*

x

x-height

x-height

The height of the letter "x"—representing the most important area of the letterform for 90% of the lowercase characters:

abcdefghijklmnopqrstuvwxyz

x-height is a more realistic measurement of the size of a typeface than point size.

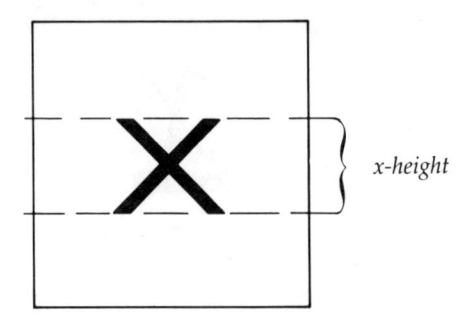

Index

Accents 2
Agate 5
Alignment 6
Alphabet Length 8
Alphanumeric, *See Font* 57
Alternate Characters 12
Ampersand 14
Arm, *See Stem* 147
Apex 15
Apostrophe, *See Punctuation* 126
Arc, *See Stem* 147
Arrows 16
Ascender 17
Asymetric, *See Symmetry* 150

Bar, *See Stem* 147
Beak, *See Stem* 147
Biform 20
Blackletter 21
Body Size, *See Type Size* 156
Bold, *See Weight* 170
Book Typography 22
Borders 24
Boxes and Bullets 25
Braces, *See Punctuation* 126
Bracketed 26
Brush 27
Bullets, *See Boxes and Bullets* 25

Calligraphy 30
Capitals 31
Cap Line 32
Carding, *See Line Spacing* 95
Character Count, *See Alphabet Length* . 8
Charcters Per Pica,
    See Alphabet Length 8
Clarendon, *See Bracketed* 26
Classified, *See Agate* 5
Close Setting, *See Letterspacing* 91
Closed 33
Color, Typographic 34
Condensed 35
Contour 36
Contrast 38
Copperplate 39
Copy Casting, *See Alphabet Length* ... 8
Counter 40
Crossbar, *See Stem* 147
Cross Stroke, *See Stem* 147
Crotch, *See Apex* 15
Cursive, *See Italic* 79
Cyrillic 41

Dashes 44
Descender, *See Ascender* 17
Didot, *See Point System* 122
Digitized Type 46

Dingbats, *See Ornaments* 112
Display Initial, *See Initial* 75
Diphthong, *See Ligature* 93
Drop Initial, *See Initial* 75

Ear, *See Stem* 147
Egyptian, *See Bracketed* 26
Ellipses 50
Emphasis 51
Expanded 52

Figures 54
Finial, *See Terminal* 153
Fixed Space 54
Font 57
Footnotes and References 58
Format 59
Fractions 60
French Modern, *See Roman* 137
French Spacing, *See Punctuation* 126
Front Matter, *See Book Typography* ... 22

Galley 62
Gothic, *See Blackletter* 21
Greek 63
Grotesque, *See Sans Serif* 140
Gutter 64

Hairline 66
Hairspace, *See Letterspacing* 91
Hanging Initial, *See Initial* 75
Hanging Punctuation,
    See Punctuation 126
Hyphenation 67

Ideograph 72
Indention 73
Inline 74
Initial 75
Inferior, *See Superior/Inferior* 149
Italic 79

Jim Dash, *See Dashes* 44
Justification 82

Kerning 84
Kicker, *See Newspaper Typography* 108

Leaders 88
Leading, *See Line Spacing* 95
Legibility 90
Letterspacing 91
Ligature 93
Light, *See Weight* 170
Line Length 94
Line Spacing 95
Logo 97
Logotype, *See Logo* 97

175

Loop, *See Counter*	40
Lowercase	98
Magnetic Ink Characters	102
Margins, *See Justification*	82
Math	103
Measure, *See Line Length*	94
Measurement, *See Point System*	122
Minus Spacing, *See Letterspacing*	91
Modern, *See Roman*	137
Mono Spaced, *See Proportional*	125
Newspaper Typography	108
Numerals, *See Figures*	54
Oblique, *See Italic*	79
Old English, *See Blackletter*	21
Old Style, *See Roman*	137
Open, *See Closed*	33
Optical Alignment, *See Alignment*	6
Optical Spacing	110
Ornaments	112
Orphan, *See Book Typography*	22
Overlapping, *See Letterspacing*	91
Outline	113
Paragraphs	116
Paragraph Symbols, *See Reference Marks* 136	
Parentheses, *See Punctuation*	126
Percent	117
Phonetics	118
Pi	119
Pictograph	121
Point System	122
Proof Marks	123
Proportional	125
Punctuation	126
Quadding	130
Quotes	131
Ragged	134
Reference Marks	136
Rivers, *See Color*	34
Rules, *See Dashes*	44
Roman	137
Sans Serif	140
Script	142
Serif	143
Set Width	144
Shaded	145
Shape, *See Contour*	36
Skew, *See Indention*	73
Slant, *See Italic*	79
Small Cap	146
Solid, *See Line Spacing*	95
Sorts, *See Pi*	119
Spine, *See Stem*	147
Spire Gothic, *See Blackletter*	21
Squares, *See Boxes*	25
Square Serif, *See Serif*	143
Stem	147
Stress	148
Stub, *See Tabular*	152
Subscript, *See Superior/Inferior*	149
Superior/Inferior	149
Superscript, *See Superior/Inferior*	149
Swash, *See Alternate Characters*	12
Symmetry	150
Tabular	152
Tail, *See Stem*	147
Tailpiece, *See Stem*	147
Terminal	153
Transitional, *See Roman*	137
Trap	154
Type Series	155
Type Size	156
Uncial	162
Underscore, *See Dashes*	44
Unit System	163
Venetian, *See Roman*	137
Vertical Setting	168
Vortex, *See Apex*	15
Weight	170
White Space Reduction, *See Letterspacing*	91
Widow, *See Book Typography*	22
Word Space	171
x-height	174

This book was input on a CCI-400 front end system and output to a Mergenthaler Linotron 202. It is set in Palatino with bold and italic.

NATIONAL COMPOSITION ASSOCIATION
A Special Industry Group of PIA, Inc.

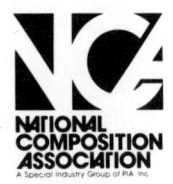

OFFICERS

Chairman of the Board
Frank J. Romano
GAMA Communications
Salem, NH

First Vice-Chairman
William A. Hohns
Waldman Graphics, Inc.
Pennsauken, NJ

Second Vice-Chairman
Larry Pleasants
Southwest Creative Graphics, Inc.
Houston, TX

Vice Chairman, Finance
Wayne Clayton
Sidney Clayton Associates
Chicago, IL

Vice Chairman, Administration
Judith Holleran
U.S. News & World Report
Washington, DC

Immediate Past-Chairman of the Board
Charles A. Lankford
Penta Systems International
Baltimore, MD

Ex Officio
G. William Teare
Byrd Pre-Press
Springfield, VA

Joseph Schiller
J. Schiller, Incorporated
Edison, NJ

DIRECTORS

Jeffrey M. Barrie
University Graphics, Inc.
Atlantic Highlands, NJ

Genevieve Bolger
Bolger Publications/Creative Printing
Minneapolis, MN

Marshall Browne, Jr.
Impressions, Incorporated
Madison, WI

Kenneth B. Chaletzky
Circle Graphics, Inc.
Winchester, VA

Calvin Cox
Maryland Composition Company
Glen Burnie, MD

David A. Dineen
AM Varityper
East Hanover, NJ

Michael McTeigue
Trandek Printing Company
Montreal, Quebec

James Oakley
Interstate Graphics, Inc.
Charlotte, NC

Adele Robey
Robey Graphics, Inc.
Washington, DC

Joel Salberg
University Graphics, Inc.
Atlantic Highlands, NJ

Richard Schiller
J. Schiller, Incorporated
Edison, NJ

Dennis R. Schonewetter
Waverly Press, Incorporated
Easton, MD

REF Z 253 .R742 1983